MW00648246

Meditation:
A Practitioner's Handbook

Copyright © 2004 Rene David Alkalay
All rights reserved.
ISBN: 1-930-32-01-4

To order additional copies, please contact us.
BookSurge, LLC
www.booksurge.com
1-866-308-6235
orders@booksurge.com

Meditation:
A Practitioner's Handbook

Rene David Alkalay

2004

Meditation:
A Practitioner's Handbook

For Swami Rama and the many masters who have transmitted the traditions of the inner school to me with infinite love and patience

MEDITATION:
A PRACTITIONER'S
HANDBOOK

Chapter I
Introductory Notes

As we begin our study of meditation, please maintain an open mind. You bring to any situation a number of preconceptions and partial or complete definitions; whatever you may have previously learned, whatever you may know of this subject, for the time that we work together, try to consider the statements in an impartial way.

Whatever your previous ideas about meditation may be, the fact that you are here suggests that you desire a deeper knowledge and understanding of the powerful laws of this practice. Your presence attests to your willingness to consider your previous information from a different perspective.

You will discover both familiar and radical statements herein, and you may even disagree with some of the statements made, but bear in mind that each statement presented comes from powerful and ancient traditions and has been the personal and universal experience of highly evolved individuals. These experiences are available to all who follow the steps necessary for their realization.

Failure to demonstrate physical, emotional, intellectual, or spiritual success in this practice is only due to imperfect knowledge of the fundamental principles. There has always been a search for shortcuts and today this approach is more prevalent than ever. But there are no shortcuts in this practice. It is an inner work, a work of the spirit. The only shortcut, if any, is from Pirkei Avot, the Wisdom of the Fathers, that states, "find yourself a teacher...." How will you find a teacher? Many are familiar with the saying that "when the student is ready, the teacher will appear." Contained in this wisdom is the statement "find yourself a teacher." *To find* means to take an active role in the process. Knowledge and wisdom arrive when we have prepared the environment for them, that is, when we are ready to receive them.

We will learn the fundamental principles with the conscious mind, but it is through practice of these principles that they will become grounded in the subconscious mind, and, thus, become a consciousness. The purpose of these talks is to develop a common language through the application of fundamental principles. It is to understand the working of the fundamental principles and to illustrate their use; and it is to develop a personal consciousness so that these principles and the practice of meditation will work automatically in our lives.

In these talks we will review several meditative traditions. After many years of practicing and teaching meditation, it has been my experience that individuality is always a factor in choosing a system or a discipline that is most effective. Some will find sitting to be the best meditative practice while others may discover the deeper levels they seek through movement. And there will be others that need to explore both of these paths toward an inner journey.

Definitions, though limited and limiting, are, nevertheless, useful and thus we will increase our language of the ancient traditions by defining the terms of our study. Each session includes didactic material for study and review, and practicum as we develop a personal meditative practice. At the end of each chapter are a series of questions designed to test your comprehension of the material and to aid you in integrating this information into the storehouse of your own knowledge.

The book you now hold in your hands is a unique educational tool. It is designed to be of significant help to you in achieving your goals. But what are your goals? We will examine this question and you will be asked to clarify or redefine the goals you have.

Meditation is both a tool and a lifestyle. As a tool, its value is determined by your proficiency in its use. As a tool also, it has little value when it is merely understood or defined. We can gain great knowledge of a particular tool. We can know its parts, its purpose, and even have knowledge of its proper use, but it will be of little service sitting idle in a tool chest. The principles and the methods will be given to you, but you must invest yourself in the process; you must be willing to do the practice consistently if you desire to realize the benefits that meditation can give you.

Meditation as a lifestyle is different from any experience you may have had. One cannot, in fact, "learn" meditation. One must take "action." This truth is manifest in all meaningful endeavors. It is the concept of karma in the East. It is the concept of tikkun in the Kabbalistic system. The value of this practice becomes evident in direct proportion to the development of this practice in your own life.

Meditation is an ancient tradition; it is a tradition that has been handed down by teacher to student, and by master to disciple for thousands of years. The program that you are beginning is very much in the mainstream of these ancient traditions; it is an old knowledge that is, nevertheless, perpetually young and fresh. As with any professional tool, it is vitally important that you use it correctly. The following suggestions will help you in your progress on the inner journey:

In order to commit ourselves to anything, we must first have a sense of its value for us. You have come to this practice because you seek something. That "something" may be an expansion of your consciousness, or it may be a desire to change your life. In all cases, you are the key element because of your desire. There is in each of us the recognition that life may hold more than we are presently getting from it, and that, given good working principles, we may discover deeper channels. So the first step is recognition. Recognizing value we take the journey seriously. It is not a practice for casual exploration. It is a practice that will have profound meaning in every area of your life.

The second suggestion is to establish and follow a schedule of practice. Spend one week on each chapter before moving on. Read each chapter once a day during this week, and follow the reading with a relaxation or meditation practice as given in the text.

We learn in a number of different ways. Among these is learning by repetitive behavior. As you repeat the study of each chapter, the material becomes incorporated into different levels of the consciousness.

As you follow your schedule, adhere to it strictly. This will give you the greatest benefits. Choose a time of day and a place where you will practice, and make these your own. This will be your time and your space for that time. If any distractions arise, see if you can place them into a different perspective. Perhaps they can be dealt with after your practice; following such a course, you may soon discover that all your activities, all your relationships begin to shift in very positive ways. In the section called "Practical Suggestions" we will review these elements.

Finally, journal your experience. Reading provides knowledge, but writing makes for exactness. Writing not only helps to organize thought, but also gives us a means by which to look back on our experience with some degree of detachment. It is a good opportunity to review and evaluate the elements in our lives. As you develop the habit of journaling your experiences and your thoughts, consider reviewing your journal notes on a weekly basis. It is a powerful tool in self-development and it will help you to reach the goals you want to achieve.

As you progress through these lessons, retain a healthy amount of skepticism. Ask questions. If something is unclear or you question its truth, research it further. The power of the inner journey is that it has no boundaries. Knowledge is infinite by its very nature. And while it is true that knowledge has little significance until we give it some boundaries, allow your imagination to expand into this work.

This inner journey and its teachings have often been the guarded practice of small groups or particular individuals. And so a misconception may exist that one must have a special talent or ability. There is the concern that we may not possess the intelligence or the personal traits necessary to activate these principles in our lives. Nothing could be further from the truth. The principles taught are universal and thus available to everyone. The human race is in the flow of evolution and we have made great leaps in technology and science. We have discovered the mysteries of the cosmos and of molecules. But there are veils through which we have not seen and that may well be beyond the experience of our senses, our language, and even our thought patterns.

If you have an inkling of the existence of another way, together with a strong personal desire, and you are willing to make a commitment to your own inner growth by following a disciplined practice, then you are indeed ready to begin the process of dynamic change and transformation.

The nature of this book is that of a guidebook; its purpose is to help you maximize your own journey, to help you determine what you want out of life, to know that the truth of abundance is an active force and that you can realize this abundance in all your endeavors.

We begin our journey with the following paradigm:

Buddha's Paradigm

Buddha sat under a Bo tree on the bank of a river watching the river. His disciples rested nearby. As he observed the river he said,

"The hardest thing is to sit."

What an odd statement, coming as it did from one of the deepest thinkers and most evolved of humans. Were you or I to make a statement like that, we might be thought to be eccentric, foolish, or just plain dumb. After all, we may ask, can I not sit whenever I choose? I am sitting, in fact, throughout much of the day. Do I need some kind of special practice for sitting?

But then, this is exactly the point. This statement is not coming from you or me. It is coming from Buddha, one of a small group of individuals of our species that are highly developed in their personal evolution. This is the historical Buddha-Gotama whose teachings represent a major contribution to world philosophy. The main body of his work is the discourses found in the Digha Nikaya (the longer suttas), the Majjhima Nikaya (the Middle collection), and the shorter suttas of the Samyutta Nimaya and the Anguttara Nikaya.

Buddha wandered from what is now West Bengal to the foothills of the Himalayas and present day Delhi. On these wanderings, he was usually accompanied by a large number of bikkhus.

Buddha was not only a great philosopher and thinker, but, according to tradition, also a master yogi, and equally versed in certain forms of martial arts. His capacity for physical postures and practices was therefore quite advanced. And so we find him sitting by a river. His bikkhus are nearby. And as he contemplates the river, he says,

"The hardest thing is to sit."

We need to look at this statement more closely, to seek its significance on a deeper level. During the course of these talks, we will discover together the meaning of this statement.

A Language for Meditation

When beginning the study of any system, the first step is to begin to speak its language. It is not necessarily important to formally learn its grammar or the correct spelling of its words, but the proper pronunciation and use of grammatical structure represents our means of communication with others and with ourselves. In philosophy, a particular language is called a "universe of discourse."

In today's world, it is common practice to clarify our understanding of a particular study in the language of a different field of study. There is a strong drive toward integration. Those individuals seeking to understand man and the universe are looking for a theory that integrates our understanding. Men of science seek a unified field theory. And yet, one of the greatest errors we can make is to try to understand one thing by the language of something other than itself. Would we think it wise to travel to Italy and prepare ourselves for communication with its inhabitants by learning to speak Chinese? Obviously, we would think anyone foolish who followed such a course. Yet, when we study the abstract systems of thought and the subtle realm of spiritual and metaphysical truth, we do this very thing.

If we are to comprehend meditation, we must learn it on its own terms. We need to learn its language. We need to do the very thing that meditation teaches us to do, to listen.

One of my teachers, Les Fehmi, said that everyone suffers from the disease called *attention deficit disorder*. Our ability to listen, to truly listen, that is to be attentive to the moment with all its subtleties, is to live in a state of awareness not usually practiced by the majority of people.

Learning the language of meditation will also require that we give some definition to this word. We will not speak in the language of ethics; ours will not be a journey into the levels of good and evil or right and wrong; these are moral judgments that we will not make. Neither is our universe of discourse the language of science; we will not understand meditation by postulates and theorems. We will most certainly draw from these, and other, fields of thought, to integrate our understanding of creation, of ourselves, and of our purpose, but the terms of meditation, its language, its grammar, spelling and pronunciations will be unique to itself.

Many questions present themselves, each requiring clarification through the understanding of terms. What is mind? What is spirit? What is soul? And what is the body? We may feel that we know the answers to these questions. Yet, it may be that we have never fully developed a clear understanding. And further, what is the relationship between mind, spirit and body?

What about our behavior? Are there not relationships between our behavior and our beliefs? Do thought, faith, prayer, and all the other mental patterns have any bearing on the state of our well-being? Although the answers seem obvious, most people have not looked deeply into these relationships and so their knowledge remains incomplete. Partial knowledge is of little use if we are to have working principles.

It is an exciting time in which science and metaphysics

have drawn ever nearer. As we continue to explore the mind, we rediscover the ancient masters who have walked along those paths before us.

Definitions

What is meditation? Well, we might begin with a dictionary definition of this word:

"To meditate is to dwell on anything in thought, to turn or revolve any subject in the mind; it is close or continued thought."

This is a beginning, but it is not enough. For our purposes, a definition of "concentration" may be even more useful:

"To concentrate is to bring to a common center or point of union; to direct toward one object by removing non-essentials; to reduce to a state of great strength and purity."

The line between concentration and meditation is, in fact, a thin but very distinct line. And to complicate things still further we have the insight of J. Krishnamurti who says,

"Any form of conscious meditation is not the real thing...A deliberate attempt to meditate is not meditation...All attempt to meditate is the very denial of it."

What a frustrating state of affairs. Here, I want to learn this ancient practice and I cannot direct my mind toward its realization. My last master, Swami Rama, taught us that *meditation is a one-pointed focus of the mind on a subtle object of concentration.* But how is this different from our understanding of concentration? It must be remembered that many definitions given by the great masters are for the purpose of opening doorways for the seeker and are not intended to be exhaustive definitions of their subject. It is our intent here to look more closely at a practice that has come down from ancient times through an esoteric tradition, and which is rediscovered by certain individuals in every place and every time.

One further statement is needed to shed light on this dilemma, and that is the phrase *"to be child-like"* in our perception of the world; now, child-like is quite different from childish, so let's be sure we are not confusing the two. Think back to your own childhood, or spend some time observing a young child at play with an object. You will discover incredible focus and concentration. In fact, a young child may spend hours studying an object from every possible angle, *revolving and turning the object in the mind.* Every thought during this extended period of concentration will be about a different facet of the object. Internalizing this process is the state of meditation.

We begin with concentration, with a one-pointed focus on a subtle object, and at some point in this concentration, a thin line is crossed into a state of meditation in which every thought, every impression, every association that arises is directly related to our object of concentration. Thus, we understand that we will learn to concentrate the mind, and the experience of meditation will take care of itself.

Concentration is one of the great laws of Thought. We need only approach our study with an open heart and an open mind, with a willingness to experiment and to discover a new country. Professional philosophers and religious leaders have shrouded this knowledge in darkness and mystery. Others have warned of its dangers. But any truth available to anyone is also available to all. Universal principles are not the restricted knowledge of special groups. They are the common property of everyone. And so it is written that Truth is a fountain of living waters.

A final definition for today is the word "relaxation." The dictionary definition of this word is minimally useful to us, and is, in fact, misleading of the technique that we will apply as it has come down through the tradition from the masters of this practice. Thus, relaxation is to relax and we find the following definition of "relax."

> ...to loosen; to slacken; to make less tense or rigid; to remit or abate in respect to attention, effort, or labor; to become loose, feeble, or languid; a diminution of tension; a remission of attention or application.

Some of this definition, namely, the part about making less tense or rigid, is quite useful for us; however, the concept of "remission or diminution of attention" is the very opposite of what we will begin to understand as the deeper process of relaxation.

Two Traditions

We spoke about a tradition. What is this tradition? There are two traditions for the transmission and incorporating of knowledge. One is the scholastic tradition, the other the monastic tradition. The scholastic tradition communicates experience by the transmission of information and the experience of others; the monastic tradition is based on our own experiential learning.

Meditation is distinctly within the monastic tradition, but there is no denial of the importance and use of the scholastic tradition. A mundane example may suffice. If I wanted to teach you about an apple, I might give a short lecture on the subject. I might explain that an apple is a fruit, that it grows on trees called apple trees, that it has certain nutrients useful to other living creatures (yes, an apple is also a living "creature"), that its skin is high in pectin and that this is good for the teeth; I might discuss the growth season of an apple and the soil and other environmental conditions necessary to its growth (i.e., there are no apple trees in a desert). And all of this information would be useful. But then, were I to ask you, "What does an apple taste like?" How would the information I have given you help you to respond? It would not be of any help. I might show you a Granny Smith apple and tell you that this apple is tart. But what is "tart?" I might show you a red delicious apple and tell you that this apple is sweet. But what is "sweet?" You see that without experiential knowledge, our learning remains incomplete. Yet, I do not intend to minimize the importance of learning by way of the scholastic tradition.

Most of us are familiar with the common cliché that "experience is the best teacher," and were anyone asked to explain this statement there is little doubt that an answer might be along the lines of,

> "Well, book learning is OK, but to really know something you have to do it."

Any number of simple examples from our life experience teaches us this truth. If you want to learn to swim, you have to get into the water. If you want to know how to fix a car engine, you have to get some grease on your hands. If you want to make an omelet, you have to break some eggs, and so on.

But was this really the original saying or intent? Well, the original saying comes from the Romans and the meaning is substantially different than our distortion of it. The Romans did indeed say that
"Experience is the best teacher..." but it did not stop there. The complete quote is:

> *"Experience is the best teacher for fools. The wise learn from the experience of others."*

Now, that is a completely different understanding than the simple contraction that we have created. So, what is scholastic learning? It is learning through received information based on experiences other than our own personal experience;

if we are selective in our choice of scholastic materials, it is information that is directly the experience of others. The words of my master, Swami Rama, however, need to be added to the above quote. He said, "this is true, but we were all fools at one time." We might reason then that the wisest among us were indeed the greatest fools. In some ways, there is some truth to this statement, but experience has shown us that some individuals appear to have a better grasp of certain forms of knowledge. Some learn from experience and are able to integrate this learning into a higher vision. It is these individuals that we generally recognize as having gained wisdom. Have they brought this knowledge with them? Are there older and younger souls?

How do we understand this idea of the integration of experience and knowledge? An important concept needs to be added to the above, and that is the idea of creative thought. It is true that we learn from others, and it is equally true that we learn by observation, personal study and experience. However, beyond the learning there is a creative process within us that first integrates all these sources of knowledge and then, by an alchemical process of the mind, transmutes them into an individual vision. A young art student may learn from a great teacher. He may spend many hours practicing his art and his craft. But after all the technique is learned, the new creation must come from within himself.

Even if a personal vision does not appear, there is, nevertheless, a difference in the craftsman's production from that of the individual who observes great art, or hears great music and says that he also will produce such work. Often at the root of this desire is the experience of seeing not only the work, but the adulation that others bestow upon the work, and upon the artist; there is the issue of fame and fortune. But these are external rewards. What have we missed with this view? We have not seen the many long hours of devotion, the personal sacrifice, the hard-won gains, and the necessary losses involved in the creation of these great works. Truth cannot receive mere mental assent; it must be practiced. It is not external, but internal.

A clear example is the healing of the sick. They pray and some are healed and some are not. We say that God has answered the prayers of some and denied the prayers of others. But is it not possible that some have prayed with deep faith and belief, and others have prayed externally with words alone. Yes, there is a longing in all, but what is the power of their thought? Does the rain fall only on fertile earth? It falls equally on earth that is fertile and earth that is barren. But from which of these soils will life spring forth? Where will the flower blossom?

Are we suggesting that we rely on thought alone for our healing? No, we are to utilize whatever is in the created world, whatever has been provided, whether it is a medical procedure, a particular medication, and laws of better living, but these alone, without the power of thought are not enough. Thought is creative, and it can create for the good as well as the bad.

Many believe in the principle of "good luck." Luck, they say, is not within our control, and so when their lives are not going well they say that they are having bad luck. And when their lives are going well, they equally attribute their success to a "run of good luck." There is some truth in the fact that some may achieve the things they want by being in the "right place at the right time." There is something to be said for "timing." But this is not the working principle that has been affective in the lives of those individuals throughout history whose lives are the very expression of the true abundance of the Universe. Even those who passively sit and wait for "good luck" must, nevertheless, be prepared to take action when this good luck comes into their lives.

In all situations we are actors or re-actors. It is generally better to be an actor on life's stage rather than a reactor to every whim and fancy that fortune places along our path.

Fundamental Principles

Standing on new terrain we would consciously or subconsciously be making mental notes as to landmarks, direction (i.e., east, south, west, north), our present location, and so on. Our landmark, our north star, so to speak, will be several premises. The first of these is that *"there is only one mind, one law, one principle, one substance, and I am one with all there is."* The second principle is that *"this law, mind, principle, substance manifests through all the myriad forms and differentiates by its use and the mechanism through which it expresses."* These premises assume that creation is a process that begins with a downward movement from above and continues in the dual process of above to below and below to above. The terms for this process are involution and evolution. We'll come back to these terms throughout this work.

This movement of energy also moves in and through us. A particular vibration coming through one of our organs of sense reaches several different levels of our consciousness. We are aware of sound with the conscious mind, but there are pathways that lead to the deeper levels of mind, the more hidden parts of the mind, and so the subconscious records the experience of the sound. Everything we see is observed, sorted, and perhaps analyzed in the conscious mind, but it is also recorded and stored in the subconscious mind. And so it is with all our senses and all impressions that come through the senses.

What is the relationship of the different levels of the mind? The conscious mind observes things sequentially; it is time and space oriented. With this mind we analyze and determine. The subconscious mind is the storehouse of memory. It is a perfect recording instrument. There is one other level of mind, and that is that mind that we call super-conscious Mind. This is that part of the mind that is the element of the Divine and the Universal. It is the repository of Hokhma, of wisdom. Wisdom, understanding and their child, knowledge are always perfect in this highest manifestation of the mind.

The knowledge of these principles, however, is of little use without the development of a practice that internalizes and activates the energy contained within them.

A Homework Assignment

Before our next session I'd like you to answer the following questions: Why meditate? What is the purpose of meditation? What will meditation do for me? What do I want to get out of meditation? Take a pad of paper and write these questions at the top of the page. Then spend five minutes a day answering these questions. Now, this is a very specific assignment so follow the directions exactly. Five minutes means five minutes. You may spend less than five minutes, but you are not to spend more than five minutes. You may feel that you are on "a roll," that you have become inspired to think and to write, and your inclination will be to keep going and write everything that comes into your mind. However, you are not to do this. If you go past five minutes you have not accomplished this assignment.

Also reflect on our brief discussion of Mind. Have we defined what the Mind is, or have we described various functions of the Mind? Do you know what the Mind is? Can you place the Mind in a particular part of the body? Within creation, the great law is change and impermanence. Is Mind also impermanent or is there some aspect of Mind that is beyond change? Buddha believed that impermanence is the cause of pain and suffering and suffering is universal. Then, in what may we find liberation from pain and suffering? What are the things that you identify with and the things that you hold onto for happiness?

As you reflect on the questions, you may answer them at any and every level you choose. You may answer them simply or in as much depth as you wish. You may answer them on a physical level, on an emotional, intellectual, or spiritual level, but only for five minutes maximum each day. Each day for the next week, during your five minutes, expand on what you have done the previous day, either by clarification of something you have written or by addition of a new insight.

A Guided Relaxation Practice

At this time we'll begin our journey toward a meditative practice with a guided relaxation. Do this practice on either a mat or a carpeted floor. I suggest that that you lie on your back with your legs about twenty inches apart and the arms at the sides of the body, a few inches away from the body; the palms turned upward, and the fingers gently curled. The eyes are closed and the focus is inward.

Bring your awareness to your breath. Without sending the breath anywhere or directing its motion, speed or rhythm, simply observe the breath. Follow the breath with your mind. Observe how it moves in the body.

Allow your body to become heavier, to sink more fully into the supporting mat or carpet. All day long gravity is working to push us down toward the earth. What acts against this force? Why are we not crushed down? It is the muscles and the skeletal system that resist this downward pressure. At this time do not resist the movement of gravity. On the contrary, let gravity work for you. Let yourself become heavier and heavier, to sink further into the supporting floor. Relaxation in a lying down position, therefore, means surrendering your body to gravity, just letting go.

Take a mental journey through the body, from the crown of the head to the tips of the toes. Systematically review each part of the body and if you discover tension anywhere, just let it go. Give each part of the body a gentle command to relax. Let the top of the head relax; let the forehead relax; relax the eyes and all the muscles around the eyes; now, relax the nose and cheeks...the mouth and tongue; let the chin relax...the jaw...the neck, shoulders and arms through to the tips of the fingers. Especially let all tension go from the hands and fingers. Allow the hands to become heavier and warmer, heavier and warmer. At this time take four slow, gentle, and complete breaths; allow the breath to be even and uninterrupted between inspiration and expiration.

With each breath allow yourself to relax more deeply, to let go more completely. Now relax the tips of the fingers, the fingers, and hands; let the forearms relax...the elbows and the upper arms; relax the chest and the upper back; let the abdominal area and the lower back relax...the pelvic area and the legs through to the tips of the toes. And take four slow, deep, even, and gentle breaths. Observe the mind. Are you still with yourself? Are you still focused within yourself in the present moment? If the mind has wandered, bring it gently back to your own center; remain focused on the breath and on deepening relaxation.

Now begin to move up through the body following the same pathway you traveled from the crown of the head to the tips of the toes. Let the toes relax...the ankles, the shins and calves; relax the thighs and the pelvic area; let the lower back and the abdominal area relax...the upper back and the chest. Let the arms relax through to the fingertips and once again take four slow, deep, even, and gentle breaths. Now relax the fingers, hands and wrists; let the forearms relax...the elbows and the upper arms; let the shoulders relax, and relax the neck and the throat; relax the jaw, the chin, the mouth and tongue; bring the awareness to the cheeks and the nose; let the eyes relax, and all the muscles around the eyes; now, relax the forehead, and the top of the head.

Bring the awareness fully to the breath. Allow the breath to be smooth, gentle, deep and even. If any distractions arise, acknowledge them but try to let them go. Remain focused and centered within yourself. Continue with this practice of breath awareness and deepening relaxation within your own silence for 3 minutes.

After 3 minutes, bring awareness back to the body by gently moving the extremities. Move the fingers and toes; open and close the hands, move the feet. Bring your hands together and rub the hands together briskly until the palms are warm. Cover the eyes with the palms and take a moment to let the warmth and darkness penetrate the eyelids. Open the eyes into the warmth and darkness of the palms, and with the next inhalation, come into a long overhead stretch; bring the legs together. Stretch the toes and flex the toes. Bring the knees up into the chest. Take the knees with the hands and gently rock the knees in toward the chest, releasing any tension that may have built up in the lower back. Roll over to your left side, and, when you are ready, come to an easy sitting position.

Sit up straight. Observe good posture. Take two or three sitting breaths and end your relaxation practice for this session. If you are doing this work in a group, ending the session with a group chant is a powerfully energizing and uplifting experience. You may use any chant from any tradition. The only caution I would offer is to use a universal chant rather than one which specifies deities or a specific religious orientation, unless you are in a closed group that shares the same religious ideas. A chant that I have found especially helpful is OM NAMO GURU DEV NAMO, "I ACKNOWLEDGE THE TEACHER WITHIN MYSELF." Chant this in the Sanskrit and repeat seven times. As you chant this, connect your energy to your own inner wisdom.

Do this practice daily during the next week, before our next session, and take a few minutes after the practice to journal your experience.

Questions for Chapter I

1. What is Buddha's statement as he watches the river?
2. Explain the term "universe of discourse".
3. Explain in your own words, the problem of understanding a subject by a language outside of itself.
4. What does Les Fehmi believe every person suffers from?
5. What is the dictionary definition of meditation?
6. What is the dictionary definition of concentration?
7. What is Swami Rama's definition of meditation?
8. What is the dictionary definition of relaxation?
9. What parts of the definition of relaxation are useful for us, and what parts are in question?
10. Explain the scholastic tradition.
11. Explain the monastic tradition.
12. What is the North Star of our universe?
13. What are the three levels of mind?

Chapter II
Kinds of Meditation

Why do we Meditate?

We ended our session last week with several assignments, so let's begin by reviewing our work. The first assignment was to answer some questions about the purpose of meditation. What is its purpose? Why do we meditate? In our group work this will be a time for sharing our insights; if you are working alone with these written materials, take the time now to review your notes before reading any further.

We mentioned several levels of the human being, namely, the physical, the emotional, the intellectual, and the spiritual. Each of these levels is affected positively by meditation. On the physical level, meditation has been shown to reduce psychosomatic complaints and to reduce stress. Emotionally and cognitively, meditators experience positive personality changes with improved self-awareness, greater self-confidence, awakened creativity and spontaneity. A heightened sense of well-being, greater energy, and better concentration are clearly observed in individuals who develop a regular meditative practice. On a spiritual level, meditation has been a doorway into higher worlds, a union with God, sammadhi, devekut, the path (Tao), self-realization, higher consciousness, and all the other terms for this experience that exist in the various traditions. Later on in this lecture, we'll consider the one word that is the purpose of meditation in every tradition, in every place and every time. Do you know what that word is? Think about it.

What about assignments two and three? How did you do with these assignments? The second part of the work was to spend several minutes daily in a self-guided relaxation practice; and the third part was to journal your experience. This is a good time to share or to review your experiences for the week.

As you develop a personal practice, review your journal notes often. You will find that reviewing your daily journal notes each evening, or the next day will begin a powerful process of self-knowledge and awakening of consciousness.

We ended our talk last week with a construction of terms and a look at two traditions of knowledge. Let's return now to the definition that meditation is the one-pointed focus on a subtle object. This needs some clarification.

Kinds of Meditation

How many kinds of meditation are there? When I have asked this question in my lectures, I have gotten back answers ranging from "one kind" to "many kinds" to "an infinite amount of kinds of meditation." I will say that there are only two kinds of meditation and that all kinds fall into one of these two categories. As soon as I say this, however, I am aware that a commitment to a fixed meaning is already problematic. Nevertheless, for the purpose of opening doorways and developing a personal practice, this may be useful.

The two kinds of meditation are active meditation and passive meditation.

It is active meditation that is defined by the words "…a one-pointed focus on a subtle object of concentration." The mind is directed to a "subtle" object and in the beginning stages of meditative practice is taught to remain with this object. The object may be a mantra or a yantra, or some combination of both. We will return to these two terms, mantra and yantra.

Passive meditation has no specific object of focus. It is to sit and observe the inner flow without attachment. It is to be fully engaged in each moment without specific focus and without a specific object. In the Buddhist tradition this process is called "mindfulness."

The two kinds of meditation are seen in the main meditative and occult traditions. Yoga and Kabbalah are active forms of meditation. There is an object, either a mantra or a yantra, or both. Buddhist meditation may be passive or active in that there may be no specific object of focus or, as in chanting, the focus may be directed.

A study is reported in which a Yogic and a Buddhist master were asked to participate in an experiment. The experiment involved each of them sitting in meditation in a sound-proof room; they were attached to neuro-feedback sensors. These are sensors that note brain-wave activity. At a given moment, a man standing directly behind them clanged a pair of orchestral cymbals together. The question the scientists sought to answer was, "will there be any change in brain-wave activity?" I'd like you to consider the question for yourself and think through the different kinds of meditation we have described. From these facts, perhaps you can discover what the difference in response was.

Remember that the Yogic adept is practicing active meditation. That is, he is focused on a subtle object of concentration and all other mind-stuff is background that is moving by like objects on a river, objects to which he is not attached. They come from beyond his view and cross before him before moving on and out of his view again. He is not attached to these objects as he remains with a focused mind on his object of concentration in the existential moment.

The Buddhist adept practicing "mindfulness" also observes the flow on the river with non-attachment. He does not have a subtle object of concentration, but he is also fully in the existential moment with every object that appears in that moment and floats away outside of that moment. What conclusions have you come to?

In order to understand the response, we need to look further within the minds of the Yogi and the Buddhist. The brain has four types of brain-waves: Beta, Alpha, Theta and

Delta. Delta is not of much concern to us in this discussion because it is the brain state that we usually associate with sleep. This is true for westerners and probably most easterners. Some Indian people, however, are in Delta state when they are meditating.

Most of the day, we are in either Beta or in Alpha. Beta is our logical, language-oriented thinking, while Alpha is associated with global thinking, that is, seeing the "whole picture. We might say that Alpha insures that we will perceive an entire forest, and Beta helps us to distinguish its individual trees. Meditation is associated with the Theta state.

In our example both masters rather quickly and easily established a Theta state and were, in fact, in deep meditation. One was focused on a subtle object of concentration while the background continued to move along; there was no attachment to the mind-stuff along mind's river.

When the cymbals were clanged behind his head, there was no disturbance because that was just another item of mind-stuff in the river's background, *regardless of its dramatic nature.* Theta waves continued undisturbed. The yogi's involvement with the existential moment through the focus on an ever-present subtle object was indeed complete.

What about the Buddhist master? There was no subtle object, or more correctly, the entire flow was the subtle object. The focus was one of "mindfulness" and non-attachment. Each moment came and went, but the ever-present existential now remained constant. When the cymbals clanged, the brain waves instantly responded by a shift toward the Alpha-Beta range, but just as quickly, when the sound passed, returned to Theta. The sound passed. There was no attachment, and the next moment was of a different nature.

Therefore, in one system there is little to no fluctuation of brain-wave activity, whereas in the other, depending on circumstance, there may be considerable brain-wave fluctuation and activity. They are different approaches on the journey toward liberation.

Buddha's Paradigm Revisited

So, now we come back to the Buddha. He is sitting on the riverbank watching the river, and he says, "The hardest thing of all is to sit." To understand this we need to look through Buddha's eyes for a moment. What is it that Buddha sees? Take yourself back to that moment in history, look at the river, and see for yourself. This is not a trick question. The question only asks about the external reality that you are now witnessing in your creative imagination. Answer this question for yourself before reading on.

What is a river? It is a large stream of water. It is not relatively stationary, as a lake might be. It is a flowing stream moving across a portion of the earth. It is a flowing stream moving to discharge itself into the sea. Is the stream clear, or are objects flowing by? Well, there are twigs, branches, sediment, rocks, fish, perhaps a boat – all these and more are flowing by and Buddha, sitting on the riverbank, says, "the hardest thing is to sit."

What Buddha recognized was an aspect of the mind. He saw in the river a paradigm that he then communicated by the analogy of "sitting." To better understand these words we turn briefly to modern psychology and literature. What is a phrase that we employ to describe the patterns of our consciousness? We speak about the "stream of consciousness." We are first introduced to this theme of the flow of consciousness in the literature of the eighteenth century novel, *Tristram Shandy*. In modern literature, we discover this stream in the works of James Joyce in his two novels, *Ulysses* and *Finnegan's Wake*. So the mind is in constant motion, like a stream. What are the objects in the stream? These are collectively called the mind-stuff. We may say that the branches and twigs are thoughts, the sediment and rocks are memories, the fish are emotions, and the boat is future plans. These are not fixed meanings; they are arbitrary selections that I have chosen simply to clarify the concept.

The patterns of our mind, like the rest of the creation, exhibit the quality of impermanence, of constant change and movement. Even our core beliefs, those thoughts we say are anchored in the depths of our mental sea, are only permanent to the degree that we maintain them. All thought is creative, that is, it leads to chains of thoughts and behaviors simply from its being. And so the Idra Suta, a highly mystical work of the Zohar asks, "Can a man put a nail into a moving wall that is about to crumble?"

There is a dilemma, a paradox, and that is that the Law of Karma speaks of a cause for every effect, or conversely, that every effect has its cause. But this very process is infinite in that each cause is also an effect of a previous cause, and each effect becomes the cause for a new effect. The process is infinite, and is infinity within the realm of creation? Is infinity subject to change and impermanence? You see the dilemma.

Now we see the relationship of the river to the mind, the objects in the river to the mind-stuff, but why is the "hardest thing of all to sit?" To understand this is to know another term in the language of meditation, and that is "the witness stance." However, even before understanding this term, we must first ask the question you thought about during the week, "What is the goal or purpose of meditation?"

The Goal of Meditation

Many answers have been given to this question. There are physical, psychological (emotional and intellectual), and spiritual reasons why different people meditate, and we've looked at these. But the goal of meditation, like the goal of Yoga, Kabbalah, the I-Ching, all world religions (setting aside their elements of power and politics), all major philosophies, all knowledge in fact – the goal of these is one. What is this goal?

The goal is **Freedom**! It is this desire that is the goal of meditation. In Yoga this is called Kaivalya Moksha and it means Liberation. In Kabbalah it is called *Devekut* and it means "to be glued to." The meaning is to be "glued to God." What is the relationship of *devekut* and liberation? Another name for God is Truth; you may remember from the New Testament, "...and the Truth shall set you free."

Just as Yoga comes from the Sanskrit word Yug, which means union, the underlying meaning of *devekut* is Union (with God). Buddha speaks of liberation from the five lower fetters. The Dhamma of Buddha is not concerned with metaphysical speculation. Buddha's teaching is eminently pragmatic; his aim is "deliverance from suffering." It is freedom. So, how can we define freedom and what has this got to do with "sitting being the hardest thing of all?"

Many Kinds of Slavery

The opposite of freedom is slavery, servitude or confinement; it is constraint, restriction and the manipulation of our free will by any force other than our Self. What are the things that control and manipulate us? Certainly outside forces control us. We can be put in prison and lose our physical liberty. We are restricted by society's laws and thus, externally, absolute freedom may indeed be a myth. But there is a deeper level of manipulation and control, and that is the control and manipulation by our thoughts and emotions. Were these thoughts and emotions within the sphere of our awareness, it might indeed be a choice for us to follow their direction. But many of the thoughts and emotions that control us are within the depths of our subconscious mind.

An example is the person who cannot hold down a job or keep a relationship. Although he or she is unhappy and often voices the desire to change these areas of their life, nevertheless, the same results continue to manifest. Why is that? What about the person who continuously argues with their husband or wife?

Day after day, on leaving work, this person says to himself,

"Today I will go home and I will not fight with my wife. Today we will have a peaceful evening. Then, shortly after arriving home an argument begins and the evening is again spent in war. What has happened? Are we so weak-willed that we say we desire a thing and then do the very opposite of our desire? Are we deluding ourselves and do we not desire at all the things we say we desire?

The answer lies in the darker recesses of the mind. While we say that we desire a thing, there is a thought pattern in the mind that is driving us in a particular direction, *whether we want to go there or not!* Consciousness is within the realm of the subconscious mind. Without the knowledge of and ability to work with this level of the mind, we are not free.

Within us is the seed of freedom. This seed may blossom into a flower, but it must receive the proper nourishment. Without good soil, without water and sunshine, without the Life-Force at its core, it may never flower. The water and the sunshine, the earth and the air is the individual on the journey of self-discovery. It is, after all, a heroic journey.

All great traditions have taught the birthright of freedom. We are in the Universe to succeed, to live lives of abundance and joy. Swamis, Rabbis, Christian theologians, Moslem priests, all have taught that there is a Divine plan and that this plan includes the abundance of the Universe. This plan includes our freedom. In our next session we will explore this relationship between freedom and the enslavement by the mind.

There are so many books written about meditation, so many courses given, and so many students studying instead of practicing. The emphasis throughout this program is on developing a personal practice. You may have wonderful intelligence and you may have accumulated great knowledge of the principles. You may even be able to teach a course on this subject; and yet you may not be getting any benefit from this knowledge, because you have not trained yourself in a disciplined manner. In this tradition, the important thing is to develop a consciousness of the principles.

A Guided Relaxation Practice

At this time we'll continue our journey toward a meditative practice with a guided relaxation. Do this practice on either a mat or a carpeted floor. I suggest that you lie on your back with your legs about twenty inches apart and the arms at the sides of the body, a few inches away from the body; the palms turned upward, and the fingers gently curled. The eyes are closed and the focus is inward.

Bring your awareness to your breath. Without sending the breath anywhere or directing its motion, speed or rhythm, simply observe the breath. Follow the breath with your mind. Observe how it moves in the body.

Allow your body to become heavier, to sink more fully into the supporting mat or carpet. Surrender your body to gravity. Just let go. Take a mental journey through the body, from the crown of the head to the tips of the toes. Systematically review each part of the body and if you discover tension anywhere, just let it go. Give each part of the body a gentle command to relax. Let the top of the head relax; let the forehead relax; relax the eyes and all the muscles around the eyes; now, relax the nose and cheeks...the mouth and tongue; let the chin relax...the jaw...the neck, shoulders and arms through to the tips of the fingers. Especially let all tension go from the hands and fingers. Allow the hands to become heavier and warmer, heavier and warmer. At this time take four slow, deep, even and gentle breaths; allow the breath to be even and uninterrupted between inspiration and expiration. With each breath allow yourself to relax more deeply, to let go more completely. Now relax the tips of the fingers, the fingers and hands; let the forearms relax...the elbows and the upper arms; relax the chest and the upper back; let the abdominal area and the lower back relax...the pelvic area and the legs, through to the tips of the toes. And take four slow, deep, even and gentle breaths.

Now begin to move up through the body following the same pathway you traveled from the crown of the head to the tips of the toes. Let the toes relax...the ankles, the shins and calves; relax the thighs and the pelvic area; let the lower back and the abdominal area relax...the upper back and the chest. Let the arms relax through to the fingertips and once again take four slow, deep, even and gentle breaths. Now relax the fingers, hands and wrists; let the forearms relax...the elbows and the upper arms; let the shoulders relax, and relax the neck and the throat; relax the jaw, the chin, the mouth and tongue; bring the awareness to the cheeks and the nose; let the eyes relax, and all the muscles around the eyes; relax the forehead, and the top of the head.

Bring the awareness fully to the breath. Allow the breath to be smooth, gentle, deep and even. If any distractions arise, acknowledge them but try to let them go. Remain focused and centered within yourself. Continue with this practice of breath awareness and deepening relaxation within your own silence for 5 minutes.

After 5 minutes bring awareness back to the body by gently moving the extremities. Move the fingers and toes; open and close the hands, move the feet. Bring your hands together and rub the hands briskly until the palms are warm. Cover the eyes with the palms and take a moment to let the warmth and darkness penetrate the eyelids. Open the eyes into the warmth and darkness of the palms, and, with the next inhalation, come into a long overhead stretch; bring the legs together. Stretch the toes and flex the toes. Bring the knees up into the chest. Take the knees with the hands and gently rock the knees in toward the chest, releasing any tension that may have built up in the lower back. Roll onto your left side, and, when you're ready, come to an easy sitting position.

Sit up straight. Observe good posture. Take two or three sitting breaths and end your relaxation practice for this session. If you are doing this work in a group, ending the session with a group chant is a powerfully energizing and uplifting experience. You may use any chant from any tradition. The only caution I would offer is to use a universal chant rather than one which specifies deities or a specific religious orientation, unless you are in a closed group that shares the same religious ideas. There are several chants that are especially inspiring for group work. One of these is to acknowledge our own inner wisdom, that is, to acknowledge that there is knowledge and wisdom within us if we only begin to listen to that inner voice. This chant is Om Namo Guru Dev Namo, and the meaning of these words is that "I acknowledge the teacher within myself."

Do this practice daily during the next week, before our next session, and take a few minutes after the practice to journal your experience. If your practice is a morning practice, review your journal notes in the evening; if it is an evening practice, review the notes sometime during the following day, preferably in the morning. You will find, over the course of a very short time, that your days begin to take on a different quality than you have experienced until now.

Remember to read through each chapter at least once daily for one week, followed by your meditation practice. At the end of your practice, journal your thoughts and experience. Meditation is indeed a treasure chest filled with precious jewels. The consistency of your practice is one of the keys by which to unlock this treasure chest. Each day, begin to live the principles that you are learning. Few of us are absolutely free or absolutely enslaved. Yet, each of us has areas of our lives that are bound by inner shackles. As you continue with this practice, observe closely how these shackles fall away and blockages in the flow of energy dissipate. The great work is more often a ridding process rather than the acquisition of more than we have.

Questions for Chapter II

1. What are the physical benefits of meditation?
2. What are the emotional benefits of meditation?
3. What are the psychological benefits of meditation?
4. What are the spiritual benefits of meditation?
5. Discuss the two types of meditation. What are their traditions?
6. Discuss the metaphor of a river in relation to the concept of the "stream of consciousness."
7. Discuss the meaning and relationship between the following: freedom, kaivalya, devekut and yoga. Discuss the idea of slavery or servitude.
8. Define "slavery".
9. Where is consciousness?
10. Why are many knowledgeable individuals unable to demonstrate the workings of universal principles in their lives?

Chapter III
The Witness

Your Practice

We'll continue our journey toward a meditative practice with a guided relaxation. Do this practice on either a mat or a carpeted floor. Lie on your back with your legs about twenty inches apart and the arms at the sides of the body, a few inches away from the body; the palms are turned upward, and the fingers are gently curled. The eyes are closed and the focus is inward.

Bring your awareness to your breath. Without sending the breath anywhere or directing its motion, speed or rhythm, simply observe the breath. Follow the breath with your mind. Observe how it moves in the body.

Allow your body to become heavier, to sink more fully into the supporting mat or carpet. Let yourself become heavier and heavier, to sink further into the supporting floor. Relaxation in a lying down position, therefore, means surrendering your body to gravity, just letting go.

Take a mental journey through the body, from the crown of the head to the tips of the toes. Systematically review each part of the body and if you discover tension anywhere, just let it go. With each breath, allow yourself to relax more deeply, to let go more completely. When you reach the tips of the toes, begin to move back upward through the body to the crown of the head. Follow the self-guided relaxation practice as you have done for the past two weeks.

Bring the awareness now fully to the breath. Allow the breath to be smooth, gentle, deep and even. If any distractions arise, acknowledge them but try to let them go. Remain focused and centered within yourself. Continue with this practice of breath awareness and deepening relaxation within your own silence for 5 minutes.

After 5 minutes, bring awareness back to the body by gently moving the extremities. Move the fingers and toes; open and close the hands, move the feet. Bring your hands together and rub the hands together briskly until the palms are warm. Cover the eyes with the palms and take a moment to let the warmth and darkness penetrate the eyelids. Open the eyes into the warmth and darkness of the palms, and with the next inhalation, come into a long overhead stretch; bring the legs together. Stretch the toes and flex the toes. Bring the knees up

into the chest. Take the knees with the hands and gently rock the knees in toward the chest, releasing any tension that may have built up in the lower back. Roll onto your left side, and when you're ready, come to an easy sitting position.

A Cognitive-Behavioral Model

So, now we have begun to learn by experience the meaning of meditation. Last week we discussed the concept of freedom. How do we understand the relationship of freedom to the mind? In psychology, there is an interesting model of psychotherapy. It is called the cognitive-behavioral model; the cognitive parts of this model were developed by Aaron Beck. Basically, the model says that we are controlled by core beliefs and when our behavior is dysfunctional, we need to explore these core beliefs. So now, you are having a problem, you go to a psychotherapist, and if he is a good psychotherapist he will follow certain steps. First, he will introduce himself and his background in order to help you to feel comfortable with his professional ability to help you. Next, there may be a phase in which trust is established within a framework of confidentiality. Now, behavior is looked at and, perhaps, beliefs may be explored. And if a belief is discovered that may be causing the problems (i.e., low self-esteem as in the belief "I am not a worthy person and therefore I do not deserve to have a good job; I do not deserve to be loved or to find love"), that belief is challenged. "Why," asks the psychotherapist, "do you think you're not a good person?" and now, the belief begins to be looked at with some distancing.

With that one question the fabric of reality has been altered. It is the magician who has waved a magic wand, the magician who has made the incantation of the secret formula, and suddenly the entire world is transformed. It may be some time before significant behavioral change occurs, but the process has begun, and once begun, unless short-circuited by denial or fear, or some other forces, it will continue.

The 32nd Path on the Kabbalistic Tree of Life is the path that unites the kingdom (the physical reality) with the reality of Foundation. It is the first path we travel in our ascent to higher worlds. The Kabbalistic teaching is that once the 32nd path is taken there is no going back. That is, once a truth is perceived we may choose to run from it or to deny it, but we can no longer remain unaware of its existence.

Non-Identification

The above principle in psychotherapy is called "non-identification with..." What is the basis for these identifications? There are many reasons for our most dearly held beliefs. Unfortunately, a good number of these reasons are the negative past experiences in our lives. Perhaps there was an abusive parent. Perhaps there was a well-meaning parent or friend who viewed us negatively and we began to see ourselves through their eyes. Our egos are a construct of these and many other influences and as long as we consider the construct as the reality of who we are, we cannot free ourselves. The experience that shaped our belief has long ago passed into the obscurity of a deeply stored memory, but its effects in our lives continue. We are unsure of ourselves. We lack self-confidence. We give up too soon, only to discover, on many occasions, that one more day, one more hour would have brought us the very thing we desired. And then, of course, there are the inevitable self-recriminations. We look at our own character traits and wonder why we are the way we are. Yet, this dissatisfaction with self is already a quantum leap forward in our journey toward self-transformation.

Without at least this basic sense that something is wrong, we cannot move forward. But there is still work to be done.

As long as we identify ourselves with the belief or the emotion, we are giving it the power to control our lives and take away our liberty. We are not free.

One more example may suffice. If I am with my children and one of my children acts in an infuriating manner, I have several courses of behavior available to me. One, I can disregard the situation totally, as if it is not happening. This is called denial, and no tradition I know of teaches the idea of this type of denial. Second, I can react with anger and strike my child or find some excessive punishment. This is a case where my anger and I are one, and so I have "acted out" my emotion. I have become my anger and my anger controls me. Third, I can recognize my anger, and maintaining my own sense of center, turn to the child and say, "What you are doing is very inappropriate. I'm going to ground you from going out with your friends for this weekend and I hope that during this time, you'll think about what you've done and why it is not the right thing to do." This last option is the expression of my anger while maintaining my separateness from it.

Now, I can hear the parents out there saying, "That's nice, but it sounds like he has no children. If he had any, he would know how hard it is to react in this way." If this is what you are saying or thinking, I agree with you. We do not always react so purely. I do, in fact, have two children and readily admit that I have not always reacted as well as I could have. But for the majority of the time, we try, and this is the way to freedom. I will not tell you that this work of self-growth is easy work. If that were the case, this might indeed be a substantially different world. Nor is meditation the only answer to many of our problems. What do I mean by this?

Is Meditation the Answer to All Our Problems?

There are so many books written about the many benefits of meditation, and we have already looked at many of these benefits. However, many of our problems need to be addressed on another level other than meditation. When we develop a meditative practice, we are not exempt from self-examination, or from confronting certain problems (when appropriate); we are not exempt from responsible action (*karma*). On the contrary, as we become better at solving our problems and dealing with the world around us, we deepen our meditative practice.

A simple example may suffice: We are given a job to do that requires specialized knowledge that we do not have. What are we going to do? Are we going to go back to our meditative space and meditate on how to do the job? What do you think? This is not a trick question. You know the answer. It is simple. You will either go out and get the knowledge that you need to do this job, or you will pass it on to someone else who possesses this knowledge. There is a third choice of course, and that is that you can be in absolute denial of your own stage of development and try to do something for which you are not yet qualified; in this case, barring the factor of sheer chance and luck, the results will probably be poor at the least and disastrous at the worst. Observe the above statement that you are "*not yet qualified.*" A key word here is "yet," because it has been my experience with many students and clients over the years that if we have the correct understanding of the uses of the subconscious mind and knowledge of universal principles, there are no closed doors. You might ask, what about individual differences? Yes, there are individual differences, but then I have also seen individuals with less native intelligence surpass those more gifted because of a better understanding of correct principles. One of my favorite sayings is attributed to Socrates, as recorded by his student and disciple, Plato. Socrates said, "The unexamined life is not worth living." You know, that statement is worth repeating. "The unexamined life is not worth living." Self-examination, self-study, study of scriptures (the wisdom of the sages), consistent practice, development of a discipline, being in touch with workable principles, willingness to acknowledge truth, these are some of the keys to living optimally.

So, what comes first, the cart or the horse? Do we meditate and improve our lives, or do we improve our lives and become better able to meditate? The answer is that each strengthens the other. But I will emphasize the importance of dealing with our problems in order to improve our ability to meditate and to get the most benefit from this practice. Perhaps the following question will clarify the concept. Do we play sports to stay in shape, or do we stay in shape to be better at sports? Again, both statements are true, but as most professional athletes clearly demonstrate, if we are to be better at the sport we need to stay in shape, to train.

Remember that meditation is one rung on the ladder of the yogic model and one element of the Kabbalistic Tree of Life; to use the yogic model of eight essential stages, we find the first four to be abstentions, observances, cultural postures and breath-work. Properly understood, these so-called "external," outer, or gross steps are as much meditative as the more inner steps of withdrawing the sense, or concentration. In fact, to practice observances and abstentions without focused attention is somewhat contradictory. As for cultural postures and Pranayama (breath control), the mind, during these practices, remains focused and centered.

This is a mind-body work that integrates these levels of our being. It is for these reasons that we do not practice yoga, for example, while watching television. It is a very different approach than the fitness model being promoted in western health clubs where at any given time you will find aerobic exercise being done (i.e., stationary bike, treadmill, stair-master) while watching a television screen or reading a magazine or newspaper. In such cases, the mind and body are in different locations.

When thought, word, and action are one, our true power emerges. This has to do with direction. Do you have a sense of direction? You may have great energy. You may have great ambitions. You may even be a gifted person with great talents and abilities. Yet without a sense of direction, none of these gifts will bring you to the life you seek. Determine your direction. This is the principle of kavannah in Kabbalah. That is, the principle of intent. What is my intent? What is my direction?

The Witness Stance Revisited

We return to Buddha's statement "...the hardest thing is to sit." Non-identification, the witness stance, the hardest thing is to sit...To observe the film script of the mind, to watch the stream of consciousness (Buddha's river), without feeling a need to be dragged along by every thought, feeling or sensation, by every distraction whether external or internal is to recognize that we are different from these things. We are not our thoughts. We have thoughts. We are not our emotions. We have emotions. We are not the sounds outside of ourselves or the sounds within ourselves. We hear these sounds. Are you beginning to understand? Internal and external things have been provided for our growth and development, and our development, in turn, acts upon these elements to transform them according to our mental patterns.

There is an assumption in this perspective, namely, that the world is not an illusion, that we and the world actually exist as separate entities. I hear your question, but what about the north star of our universe, what about the statement that all is one? That is the paradox of transcendence and imminence. Transcendence is to go beyond all limitations. It is the quality beyond all human knowledge. Transcendence is that reality beyond the creation, the unlimited reality that contains the limited universe. In Kabbalah it is called the light outside of man expressed in the two qualities of soul: Khaya and Yehida. Immanence is also a quality beyond human knowledge; our best perception of this concept is the light within the creation, the light within man as expressed in the three qualities of soul: Nefesh, Ruakh, and Neshama. A fuller description of these Kabbalistic concepts may be found in my book *Three Paradigms*.

In order to unify the opposite energies in the universe, to bring together matter and spirit, we must recognize their existence. In regard to matter, there is no difficulty. We perceive matter through our senses. Matter occupies space. It has physical substance and this is the densest form of experience. But what of spirit? This is not quite that easy for us. We conceive of spirit as a vital force, as an immortal part of the universe. In order to experience the spirit we begin with the breath, the vehicle of immortality. We begin as fools and, by experience, develop varying levels of wisdom, each individual according to his means and his circumstance.

It is perhaps the hardest thing of all, to sit and observe the flow of mind-stuff in a spirit of non-attachment, yet fully focused and aware. How many times have you sat at your desk working on a job when you suddenly realize that you have not been there at all for the past several minutes? A chain of thoughts, a group of twigs and branches, has pulled you along down the river. Or have you been on a date with someone over dinner or lunch and suddenly realize that they have been speaking but you have not heard a word they said for the last few sentences? Where have you been? A chain of feelings, a school of fish, has pulled you away from attentiveness to the moment.

There are two issues here. First, is the idea that we are other than the things we carry around with us; and, second, are the things themselves that we carry around. One of my early teachers, Vernon Howard told the following story:

The Man with the Pumpkin on his Head

A traveler is walking down a country road toward a village. He is clearly staggering under a great load. In his right and left hands he holds large rocks. On his back is a knapsack filled with dirt, rocks and broken twigs; around his waist there are coils of seaweed; on his head is a very large pumpkin.

As he staggers down the road, he meets a villager coming toward him. The villager greets him and then asks, "Why are you carrying such big rocks in your hands?" The traveler looks at the rocks and observes on the strangeness of the situation. He says, "I never really noticed them before." And he proceeds to throw them away.

He continues on his way and meets another villager who asks, "What are you carrying in your backpack; it seems especially heavy?" The traveler removes the backpack, opens it, and, finding it filled with dirt and rocks, discards it.

The next villager asks about the seaweed and that is promptly discarded. Finally, another villager comes along and asks our traveler, "Why are you carrying such a large pumpkin on your head?" The traveler removes the pumpkin and stares at it for a while; then, he says, "I didn't know what I was doing to myself." He then threw away the pumpkin and continued toward the village. He was no longer staggering under his burden. His step was easy and light. What do you think this traveler's problem was?

Well, he had two problems. The first was that he was carrying around a lot of extra baggage, a lot of unnecessary baggage; but his bigger problem was that he was not even aware of the extra unnecessary burden he carried. Once he was aware of the extra load, he was only too ready to let it go. This story is, of course, simplistic, but it does make the point that freedom is a ridding process, a lightening of the load of negative emotions, of jealousies and hatreds, of greed and avarice, and all the other "useless" qualities that diminish our humanity. In the course of our lives, however, it is not quite so easy to discard negative behaviors, even after we become aware of them. Cognition alone does not guarantee that behavior will change. There are extra steps that we need to take. Nevertheless, without the awareness that something is indeed wrong, a turning toward another way is not possible.

There is a relationship between freedom and wholeness. It is discovered by the process of a one-pointed focus on a subtle object – attentiveness in the existential moment. A story is told by the philosopher Bertrand Russell. He relates that his wife was very social and attended many social gatherings, and she often requested that he attend these events with her. He, on the other hand, found these gatherings boring and a waste of time, and he never enjoyed himself. Then, one day it dawned on him that a reason he was not enjoying himself might be because his body went with his wife, but his mind stayed at home where he preferred to be. He determined that the next time they went to one of these social functions, he would take his mind along. And, well, you can guess the rest of this story...he discovered that these functions or gatherings were not really bad at all.

Freedom is the state of being free. It is exemption from

slavery, from any manipulation external to the self. To develop the ability to observe our mental processes without a need to identify with them, to observe them without being pulled along by them, may well be the hardest thing of all. It is to look within and cast light on areas of the psyche that are in darkness. It is to rid oneself of unnecessary burdens and to be engaged in the moment as whole beings.

Our approach to meditation will be that of the scientist-mystic. There is a method and if this method is followed, the experience of others who have followed this method will also be attainable by us. Think clearly about your direction. Recognize your essential nature as different from the many constructs that make up the ego. Follow your discipline and persevere – the prize, remember, goes to him who finishes the race. Choose and become an actor rather than a reactor. Review the gifts you have been given and recognize that you must act, you must perform karma. We cannot escape the performance of karma, but it is within our choosing to determine the karma, the actions that we will perform.

A Sitting Practice

We'll begin today's session with a sitting practice. Sit either in a straight-backed chair or on the floor. If you are sitting on a chair, let the thighs be parallel to the floor. In order to accomplish this, it may be necessary to place cushions under the feet, or to place a cushion on the seat of the chair. In either case, sit away from the back of the chair; sit up straight with the hands, palms down, on the knees. Keep the shoulders down and relaxed. The chin is approximately in balcony position, that is, parallel to the floor. The legs are comfortably about hip distance apart.

If you are sitting on the floor, the legs are crossed creating a triangular base with the torso as a foundation. There is no need to have the legs in any special crossed position. Whatever is comfortable and will allow you to sit quietly will do. As above, the same principles apply. Sit up straight, observing good posture. The hands, palms down, are on the knees. The shoulders are down and relaxed. The chin is approximately in balcony position, that is, parallel to the floor.

Whatever your sitting position, whether on the floor or on a chair, close the eyes and begin to focus your awareness on the breath at the point between the upper lip and the nostrils. Do not send the breath anywhere or direct its course in any way. Simply observe it, follow its course through your body, recognize and affirm the process of the breath.

Now let's refine this practice. As you continue to sit, you may become aware of certain physiological responses. For example, you may become aware that the legs are falling asleep or have begun to ache. Bearing in mind the phrase "comfortable extreme," disregard any discomfort on the part of the legs and continue to sit focusing the awareness on the breath. The legs and feet will habituate to the posture and the discomfort will diminish and eventually disappear.

Next, observe the muscles in the back. These may have begun to ache. Again, this is because the muscles in your back may have lost the habit of holding you in a good posture. If this is the case, then once again disregard any temporary discomfort. Your muscles will habituate to holding you upright and this discomfort will disappear.

In both of the above instances, the necessary response was to do nothing. Are there aspects to this practice that require intervention? The answer is, yes! One of these is the observation that your body has begun to sag down. Remember, gravity in this case is not working to help you remain upright; gravity is pushing you down and the only things that are holding you up and keeping you from being crushed by the force of gravity are the muscles and bones. If you observe that you have begun to sag down, lift yourself back up to a straight sitting posture.

Finally observe the eyes. If you find any movement there, still this movement consciously. The eyes are very close to the brain; there are very direct pathways between the eyes and the brain. Movement in the eyes generally indicates movement in the brain, and this movement may be said to indicate restless and unfocused activity. As you still the eyes, you are sending a direct message to the brain to become a little quieter.

Having taken these steps, take a moment now to make a

brief mental commitment to yourself to be in your present space and time. Begin to listen to all the sounds from outside your space. Spend thirty seconds to one minute listening to these sounds (or no sounds, whatever the case may be); now, listen to the sounds inside your space. Spend thirty seconds to one minute listening to these sounds. Next, bring the sound closer to yourself and listen to the sound inside your own ears. Continue with this awareness for thirty seconds to one minute. Now bring the awareness fully to the breath. Allow the breath to be silent, but listen to its sound inside your self.

As you continue with this practice, acknowledge all distractions, whether external sounds like phones ringing, doors opening, people speaking, trucks or cars zooming by, and so on, or internal sounds like thoughts or feelings. Acknowledge all these without feeling a need to be drawn away by them. Acknowledge them, but remain with your focus on the breath. If you find that the mind has wandered from breath awareness, as soon as you become aware of it, gently bring the mind back to your center, to your focus.

Continue with this practice within your own silence for a period of five minutes.

What was your experience? Did your mind become empty? Much of this teaching was guarded and passed down within a limited community of initiates. The information just wasn't universally available. Today the situation is quite different. The esoteric teachings are readily available, but the information explosion has led to a great deal of misinformation alongside the "real thing." Many books on meditation, for example, discuss this idea of "emptying" the mind of thought. I realize that you may not be experienced at meditating, but let me ask you what you think of this idea. Do you think that you can empty your mind of thought? I'm going to go out on a limb here and say that you cannot. The issue is not one of emptying the mind; it is about stilling the mind. In this stilling process, a deep quiet is experienced, a kind of stilling of the waters. In this condition, reflections are not distorted and the hidden roots of reality in the upper worlds may be realized.

Passing beyond the reflections is to transcend briefly the boundaries of human perception. The world around us is, after all, not limited to the reality of human perception. We know from our scientific investigations, that the Universe is made up atomic and subatomic particles; electromagnetic fields are constantly operative; gravity is the fundamental law in the relationship of objects; we learn about dark space and string theory and the many other realities that are not available to our senses. Our senses are functional within a certain range; it is not a range that allows us to perceive matter on particle level. Many other of earth's inhabitants (i.e., bats, fish, reptiles) respond to light and sound frequencies that are not a part of our reality.

Can we "see" beyond the limitation of our senses? Certainly we can reason beyond our senses. If this were not the case, we would not have formulated the many theories about unseen laws that operate in the Universe. But the question here is can we "see" beyond our senses? Is there another level of sense perceptions that is available to us? When we experience or perceive through our five external senses, we have a verbal construct that approximates our perceptions. When we reason and think we also have a verbal construct to express our abstractions. The experience of meditation, however, is one in which we do not have an adequate language. It is not an experience that lends itself to intellectual explanation. Yet, as with any scientific method, it has the quality of duplication. If one follows the "scientific" steps necessary for the realization of this experience, there is a long and well-documented history of millions of individuals who have reproduced this inner "perception."

The issue of fact or fiction is indeed relevant. In this "science" we remain cognizant of the perceived object and the perceiver as subject. Because of this perspective, all truth, all "reality" will contain the colors of individual vision. There is no way to understand the personal vision of another creature. Whatever is expressed will of necessity be a limited portion of that vision. The reason for this is because of what was said earlier, the inadequacy of language to convey certain levels of experience. It is, therefore, not in their particulars that we confirm the experience of meditation of others, but in their generality.

Our practice is not about finding answers. On the contrary, it very often leaves us with more questions. As we connect more deeply with the reality of external perception in relation to internal awareness, we discover that the mind is much more than the neural mechanisms of the brain.

Questions for Chapter III

1. When developing a sitting practice, what are two possible circumstances that would require intervention?
2. When developing a sitting practice, what are two possible circumstances that are to be disregarded?
3. In what way can we utilize gravity as an ally in this practice?
4. Why is it important to make a mental commitment?
5. What is the meaning of freedom?
6. The traveler had two problems. What were the traveler's two problems?
7. Explain the relationship of internal and external things to the self.
8. What is Socrates' statement about self-examination?
9. In what way do we handle distractions during meditation?
10. Who was Aaron Beck and what is the basic premise of the cognitive-behavioral model?

Chapter IV
Ritual

An Orderly Universe

We begin our session with a sitting practice as in our previous session. Observe the physical elements and the mental commitment. And then continue with the practice of breath awareness for ten minutes.

Over the next few weeks we will talk about practical tools for developing a meditative practice. In order to understand the importance of a practice that follows a very definite order, it is necessary to understand the uses and importance of ritual.

Ritual is a part of our lives in every major life-situation. Birth is a ritual in the way the newborn infant is brought into the "tribe" of his or her people. Jewish and Moslem male children are circumcised. A Christian child is baptized. All peoples have some ritual surrounding childbirth and the welcoming of a new soul. Marriage is a ritual. Death is a ritual. There are rituals called rites of passage. A corporate board meeting is a ritual. Greetings and farewells are rituals. Everything that follows a set order may be understood as a ritual. In that sense, our galaxy is in a ritual cosmic dance, as are all the other galaxies. The entire Universe, following a set order, is working its way through a ritual. Developing a meditation practice is also to develop a specific ritual.

The above statements take the understanding of ritual far beyond a dictionary definition. The dictionary understands ritual to be specifically related to religious observance. Thus, we read that ritual is based on the word "rite," and a rite is a

> *...formal act of religion or other solemn duty.*
> *A religious ceremony or usage; ceremonial.*

and ritual:

> *...pertains to rites; consists of rites;*
> *and is the manner of performing divine services.*

This definition is only useful to the extent that the dance of the universe may be viewed as a divine service. When we perform a ritual correctly it connects us to energy much greater than ourselves. This is its mystery and its power. When actions, thoughts and speech are in harmony, the potential for an individual to achieve his or her goals is dramatically expanded.

A Hidden and a Revealed Dimension –Tefillin

Everything has a hidden and a revealed dimension. In Kabbalah the terms for these two dimensions are niglah (revealed) and nistar (hidden). As an example we'll take a ritual action from the Jewish tradition; any tradition will do, and after the examples given here you may wish to discover their application to ritual within your own tradition. So, we find that a Jewish man, upon arising, places upon his head and upon his arm phylacteries, or tefillin. They are made of leather as are their straps. Inside the phylacteries, there are specific prayers. These prayers are the prayers of the Sh'ma, the great mantra of unity of the Jewish people. The words of this mantra are, "Hear Oh Israel, God is our God, God is ONE. It is an affirmation of the simple unity of God and the simple unity behind creation. It is an affirmation that this unity is available to us (God is *our* God), and, in this context, all people have access to the spiritual Israel and the unity (*devekut*) with God. Further, the phylacteries must be wrapped in a very specific manner around the arm and hand, and placed on the head.

What is the meaning of *tefillin*? We are to wear *teffilin* on our head and bind them on our arm. One goes on the head and must be on the forehead at the hairline; it must be centered, and the back knot must rest at an exact point at the back of the head. The other is bound on the arm, over the bicep, adjacent to the heart. The strap is then wound seven times around the forearm and the process is completed with a very specific pattern around the hand and fingers. Inside the *tefillin*, certain prayers must be written and no others will do. And we are to recite specific prayers and blessings upon donning these unusual objects.

There is a *niglah* and a *nistar*, a revealed and a hidden meaning. The *niglah* of *tefillin* is rather obvious; it is the symbol that *tefillin* represents. Putting on the *tefillin*, like so many ritual actions in a religious context, remind us of our spiritual nature, of a power greater than our own and our faith in the workings of this power in the Universe, and of the necessity to elevate ourselves in all our dealings with the world around us. Thus, when I leave my home for the battles of the day, I enter the battleground as a child of God. I am to deal with others fairly, with justice, and with ethics. And when I return to my home, I am to leave the "dust of the earth" outside and enter my home as a spiritual being, to remember to act with my wife and my children with fairness, truth and ethics.

But what is the *nistar* of *tefillin*? Why, for example, must they be made of leather? I am an ethical vegetarian. I have a problem with this. Can I not get *tefillin* that are made of some other material? Why are they worn between the eyes, at the place of *ajna*, the sixth chakra, the third eye, and on the arm adjoining the heart? Why must they be wrapped seven times around the arm and then in a very specific pattern around the hand? Why must the knot at the back of the head fall just at one particular spot? What about the prayers that are contained within the *tefillin* – can they not be other prayers and be just as effective? Why must these prayers be written on parchment by a scribe? Suppose I were to get a computer program to print out thousands of such little scrolls with those particular prayers. Wouldn't this be more economical? Some of the above elements have, of course, been answered by rabbinic commentaries. For example, we bind them between our eyes and next to our heart to indicate our full acceptance of the Divine laws that are operational in the Universe. We acknowledge the sacred and we accept our unique relationship to it.

This speaks to a basic tenet in the esoteric traditions. All the great masters, teachers and initiates from every tradition have maintained what at first appears to be an untenable paradox, namely that free will exists, but that personal free will does not exist. However, there is no paradox here. It is the awareness of a Primal Will in the cosmos and the more we become attuned to this Will, the more we become vehicles for its manifestation.

The development of this consciousness is not easy. It requires work and commitment. But here is a most unique concept for such an esoteric idea. As you realize these principles as working principles in your life, they become a new set of habits that have replaced an earlier way of thought. For every birth there is a death. For new ideas to be born, old ones pass away. It is the inner and the outer cycle of life.

A Hidden and a Revealed Dimension – Mezuzah

Rabbi Schneerson, the last *rebbe* of *Chabad*, taught that the *mitzvah*, the commandment, of the *mezuzah* was an even more direct expression of this behavioral imperative. For those unfamiliar with this term, a *mezuzah* is that object that may be seen on the doorpost of every observant Jew's home, and for those who take this commandment very seriously, there is a *mezuzah* that is placed on the doorpost of every room within the house. It is specifically placed on the doorpost of the door that leads out of and into the home. This is because we are to kiss it on leaving the home and on entering the home. The *mezuzah* has a very clear symbolic meaning, as well as aspects that are not easily comprehensible. For example, the ritual of *mezuzah* also must follow exact steps in order to be valid and effective. It must be on a particular side of the doorway; it must be at a certain angle. The *muzzuzah* contains the prayers of the *Sh'ma*; it must be written on a scroll and it must be handwritten by a scribe.

Here are the questions then. Why, for example, can I not simply write in my journal that I want to be more spiritual, to live in the world with ethics and justice, to love all God's creatures, great and small? And if not my journal, or daily planner, why not ask a friend to remind me about these things daily? Or, what about hiring a service to call me each morning and each evening and tell me to be more spiritual? More to the point, what if I perform the prescribed action, but change its order, or omit one step? Is it so important? Isn't it more important that I understand the significance of the action and focus on its intent?

We enter a workshop to accomplish a particular goal, to produce a particular creation. So, I enter my carpenter's workshop to build a table, but I must know the nature and the use of my tools; I must have experience in the handling of these tools. Without this knowledge and skill, and following the designated steps, would I produce the creation I wanted to produce? In fact, would I produce anything of value and would I not be at some risk of injury from the tools themselves?

This is the realm of the conscious mind. We consciously choose, and we consciously make a commitment based on our intent. Yet, even this conscious intent, becomes a subconscious force working on our behalf beneath the surface of awareness. The idea of *thought being one* is the harmonious cooperation of all levels of the mind. In conjunction with speech and performance (action), they are the elements that transform the mundane to the dynamic. In the practice of these principles, there is no such thing as an average individual.

It is one more of the paradoxes of this work that we have a purpose for entering the meditative practice and yet we are to have no purpose if the meditative experience is to be accessed. This is indeed a dilemma. In this work, we will take the approach that we practice concentration and meditation for the purpose of connecting our energy with a higher energy, of connecting the self with the Self, the microcosm with the macrocosm, of experiencing the oneness beyond the myriad external forms. Does the process work without intent?

Kavannah

The last question is perhaps the hardest. Are we to act with intent? The name for intent in the sytem of the ancients of Israel is *kavannah*, and the answer to this question of *kavannah*, intent, is yes and no. Yes, to act with intent and with understanding of the significance of our actions is to infuse the action with more powerful energies. No, to perform an action with intent, but to leave out steps is to render the ritual action ineffective. Part of intent is a focused determination of the purpose of our practice. Why do we meditate? Intent supports our affirmation that only the object of our focus will be held in the mind. Intent is the motivation to prepare the body.

Intent is the secret ingredient that equalizes individuals of varying abilities. We often believe that we do not have the talent or the ability to achieve a certain thing. We think to ourselves that if we only had a certain talent, certain doors will open for us. There is, of course, some truth to this idea. King Solomon wrote "And your gifts will bring you before great men." But it is equally true that the so-called average person may excel beyond the more gifted person. It is a matter of correct usage. Many gifted individuals dissipate their gifts by their misuse. Whereas someone with lesser gifts may use them more optimally and thus discover that his dreams are within his reach. Set high goals. Do not fear setting high goals. Have faith in your ability to achieve these goals. Maintain a positive attitude. You will discover strengths within yourself that have always been there. No one has given these to you. They came with the program. You have only to discover their existence and allow them to manifest in your life.

So now we understand the symbolism and the concepts involved. In literature, we are presented with a number of forms, such as similes, metaphors, and allegories, and we find that the symbol is the deeper meaning of a particular writing. In the esoteric traditions, the symbol is actually the first level in. The deeper level is *nistar*, the hidden dimension of a thing. Let us try to answer the question now. Ritual is based on the order that makes up its parts. What do I mean? A ritual has distinct steps for its fulfillment, and if we change any of these steps, the ritual may be invalid and ineffective. Why would this be so?

Do You Know the Ritual of Credit Cards?

Ritual connects our energy to a much higher energy source, and if any of the steps of the ritual are altered or left out, the chances of making that connection are fundamentally non-existent. We do not easily accept this because many of us believe that *"we are the only reality"* and therefore ritual performed in any way we choose will be valid and effective. This could not be further from the truth. Anyone examining this statement closely and considering its full meaning will realize that ritual must be exact.

Some examples will clarify. Do you own a credit card? I will assume the answer is yes, only because we live in a world of plastic and everyone seems to have a credit card. Now, you go into a store to make a purchase and the salesperson asks, "How will you be paying for this?" You take out your credit card and pass it over to the salesperson. The salesperson then makes out a receipt, swipes your card through a little square-shaped machine, and the machine gives back a message; that message is "accepted," rejected," or "call for verification," or some other message. A question then: is it the little box that gives you the credit? The answer is obviously "no!" That little box connects to a much larger "box," or system, and it is the larger box that sends back the message through an intricate network of cable connections. If that salesperson were to swipe your card through that little machine in any way other than the correct way, the machine would not be able to give back a message *because it could not make the connection.*

Remember, we have said that if you follow certain steps, a connection will be made. It is not so because of external powers. Many believe that if they call upon a deity to grant their wishes, if they dance in a certain way, or chant a particular chant, rain will come, or the wind will change its direction. Christians use rosary beads; Hindus use *mala* beads; here is a further example of intent, of kavannah, and its importance in the practice. Yes, the ritual steps may, in fact, bring some type of response, but the deeper power of these ritual steps, and the results obtained are just as often dependent on the individual and his or her development. In the course of personal development, understanding of the principles deepens and the individual works in harmony with universal law.

This is the meaning of the rabbinic saying, "If you make God's will your will, then God will make His will your will." All the great adepts have understood this principle.

Certainly, some of the earliest rituals we find concern themselves with the death and rebirth of the earth. Early human societies gathered their harvest and then, for some, faced bleak and harsh winters. The winter was a time when the earth seemed to die. And then, of course, came the spring when buds appeared but food did not yet become fully accessible. For these early societies, this ritual was literally a matter of life and death. All early gods had symbolic relation to the earth: Osiris was a god of the wheat; Dionysus was the god of the fruit tree.

Misunderstanding has led to widespread misuse of these fundamental laws. Thus, among all native people, some form of sympathetic magic has been practiced. Such practice is founded on the principle that "as above, so below," namely that like will produce like. Therefore, if a result is desired, an action needs to be taken that is like the result being sought. Although this idea has been used to develop fantastical ceremonies and practices, there is, at its core, the very sound idea that we attract to ourselves those energies with which we are in harmony. It is a matter of consciousness. If I want good health, I must have a consciousness of health; this consciousness will express itself in my life-style choices and draw to me the thing I desire. If I want wealth, I must develop a wealth consciousness. It may happen that individuals will achieve these and other conditions without any particular affinity for them, but those would be exceptions to the principle. In such cases, there may be a factor of chance, but this has never been the path of those individuals in history who have reached their goals and realized their dreams.

It is, however, not as simple as saying that if you will do a certain thing, a certain result will come about. Ours is not the only will in the universe. And even in the expression of our will, do we know ourselves so well that there is no division between our thought, word and action?

The simplification of this idea is to assume that we perceive the cause and effect relationship of a thing. There is much to be said for the idea that if we do a certain thing, a certain result will follow, and its corollary, that if we do not do a certain thing, we avoid a bad consequence (i.e., "...of the fruit of the tree of the knowledge of good and evil, ye shall not eat...- or you'll have to leave the Garden of Eden). Yet, in the forms that this principle is applied, there is little more than superstition and fantasy.

A mother is giving birth. The labor is difficult. A tribal doctor is with her. Outside the house, another tribal member has tied a large rock to his stomach and is lying on the ground, moaning in pain while simulating the expectant mother's delivery. This simulation of the birth will continue until the actual birth is completed.

A hunter is going out to hunt for the tribe. No one in the tribe will touch oil until his return. This abstention is not for the purpose of mortification. It is a statement that the hunter will have good fortune and that the animal will not slip through his hands.

Do You Know the Ritual of the Telephone?

The impression might be that, regardless of what has been said about the importance of following precise steps, it is more important to understand the inner meaning of the principles. The truth is that both are important. We'll use two more examples to emphasize the importance of exact steps, the "telephone." You step into a phone booth and call your friend. However, you have forgotten one of the numbers and so you take a chance and punch in the missing number. The number, however, is wrong and you cannot make the connection that you want. No matter how often you dial, until you use the correct number the connection will not take place. In fact, there is the further difficulty that even if you have all the right numbers, they must be entered in the correct order; should you exchange the positions of any two of the numbers, the connection here also would be unavailable. Do you understand how these examples address the question of nistar and ritual?

Do You Know the Ritual of the Human Physiology?

The human physiology is a ritual of parts working harmoniously. Suppose we take a person apart and put him back together with parts in different locations. The statement itself is ludicrous, and it is quite obvious that if we put the heart where the foot is, and substitute the stomach for the brain (a substitution that many unfortunately actually make), and continue to so re-arrange the human anatomy and physiology, it is readily understood that the arrangement of parts would not function. The Gestalt model is correct in stating that the whole is greater than the sum of its parts, and those parts must be in their correct order.

A criticism often voiced by metaphysicians is that the performance of a ritual is based on a false idea, namely, that some power external to us will grant our wishes. And the statement is further made that we need to look within and not outside ourselves. There is a problem with these suppositions. There is an assumption that the external and internal are radically different; this is not to perceive the immanence of the Divine in every molecule of creation; and second, is the assumption that there is no God outside ourselves, and this is not to see the transcendent aspect of the Divine outside of the creation. The other fallacy of this thought is that we perform a ritual in order for an outside agency to grant us a wish. That is not the purpose of ritual.

Ritual, as we have seen, is operative on several levels. First, on a physical level, it joins people into a community through shared customs. Mentally and emotionally, it assures societies of the continuity of common values. And spiritually, it connects us to the universal laws that are the very core of creation. Some years ago I sat in on a workshop with the English Kabbalist, Z'ev ben Shimon Halevi and he made a wonderful statement about ritual,

> "The essence of ritual is that something done in the physical realm is related to the higher worlds. This may be a simple gesture of the hand or an elaborate ceremony. It can be working consciously in everyday life so that quite mundane actions become full of meaning, or a carefully designed ritual acted out for a specific occasion. It (ritual) is the formalizing of action and giving it not only meaning, but creating a contact with other worlds."

In this period of world history, the twentieth and now the twenty-first centuries, change is occurring rapidly. Values and mores are shifting faster than our ability to keep up with them. Information has shifted from something that we once had to work to get, to a situation in which we are glutted with information; our challenge today is not about acquiring information, but to sift through all the information and weed out the misinformation. And we find ourselves polarized in our emotions toward longing for the stability of established rituals on the one hand, and denying the validity and meaning of these rituals and wanting to either create entirely new ones or to discard this aspect of behavior completely. When we review these options, we are left in greater confusion than ever because none of these options seem right to us. It is a dilemma and we seek in so many ways to find the solution. Psychotherapy has not helped us. Science has no solution. In many ways these leave us feeling more isolated than ever, either in the cult of individuality or the perception of our microcosmic existence in the vastness of creation. We fall into the dark holes in the Universe. We dissolve into the particles of particle theory.

There is light at the end of this tunnel. We are in a period of transition and all transitions are difficult. As we spin through space together, rituals are being reaffirmed and infused with significance by a generation that is discovering, or perhaps rediscovering their inner meaning. And so we take the rituals that have become rote for so many people and give them new life through the two aspects of renewal (seeing them in the spectrum of our time and place) and kavannah, intent. It is not a coincidence that we find the "renewal" movement in our century.

Looking back to humanity's earliest rituals what is most apparent is their functionality. Although we can formulate some concept of rituals, it is their level of nistar for which we ultimately have no language, and thus we surround ritual with myth. There are anthropomorphisms of gods and goddesses, of magical animals and fantastic creatures. The acting out of these early myths is the beginning of theater. And so, step by step, we move further from the real significance of our arts, the annual renewal of life.

The Significance of Parts

A ritual, to be valid, must have certain parts, and it must follow a certain order. If properly followed, the ritual connects us to the source of creation and to the center of our being, to the self. There is an additional note of some importance and that is the question whether there is only one way to do these things. It appears that what is being said is that we must follow traditional rituals in order to access the meditative, mystical or religious experience. The answer is clearly no; there are other ways. To believe otherwise is to believe that the realm of knowledge and wisdom are fully explored and that we have closed all doors to explorations of the mind. You have the possibility of discovering a new structure by which to access the experience we are discussing. However, that new structure will, of necessity, be in harmony with universal principles and laws. What we are saying is that the pursuit of this knowledge is established through time-tested methods, methods that we refer to as ritual, and that if we follow these methods, the experience of meditation is available to us.

The Ritual Guidebooks

There is a great deal of negative reaction to the study of scripture; yet swadhyaya, self-study, is defined by the great Yogic sage Vyasa as the recitation of the OM mantra, the Gayatri mantra, and study of scripture. He goes on to say that swadhyaya leads to illumination and liberation (kaivalya).

Holy scriptures of any people are ritual guidebooks and need to be understood in this way. The Torah is a book that says, in short, "follow my teaching in all its ways and particulars, and you shall inherit the land; each man shall sit under his own olive tree..." The Bible, and ritual in general, however, with its many rules and regulations appears to many as a great burden. The yamas and niyamas of the yogic system are guides to the way we are with others and the way we are with ourselves. Thus, we find that lying and stealing, as well as the other yamas, are behaviors that are said to pollute the mind. The objective of the yamas and niyamas is, in fact, to cleanse the mental body. But we feel that we know how to live and isn't it some nerve that someone else wants us to do things his or her way. What nerve, what *chutzpah*, we say.

A Man and His Boat

To understand this, let us imagine a man who enjoys the sport of boating. He purchases a boat for $20,000 and he takes his new boat out to sea. Before departure, he sits down and reads through the manual of instructions that came with the boat. Now it just so happens that the instructions are full of "don't do this" or "don't do that." Don't drill a hole in the bottom of the boat. Don't leave the harbor until you've checked on the workability of your instrumentation. Never pull the red handle hanging down from the overhead compartment. Would our new boat owner consider this nervy on the part of the manufacturer? Would it ever dawn on our man to say "I bought this boat. I paid $20,000 for this boat. If I want to drill a hole in the bottom, I will just go ahead and do that. If I want to leave the harbor without any working instruments, that is nobody's business but my own."

Of course he is right. If he wants to do those things, it is his boat for now, and he can indeed do exactly as he has said (this also leads to deeper questions that are neither so clear cut regarding true ownership) . But that is not the point for now. He is setting out in his boat in order to have a good experience. He wants the boat to operate correctly. He does not want to sink his boat or to sink with his boat. He does not want to be lost on the high seas. And so he reads the "guidebook" and follows its directions because he knows that it has been written with him in mind. It has been written to make his trip a better trip, one that will optimize his experience.

Read the scriptures of your people, whatever your tradition, and you will find great wisdom there. Review the principles that have been handed down and determine for yourself if there is not a better way to live, one that optimizes the journey. As the body and mind are cleansed, blocked energies are released, and we reach into the higher realms of being.

This is the deeper meaning of ritual and of scripture. Until a glimpse of the truth is gotten, the practice of sitting quietly for a certain period of time each day may seem quite prosaic; however, it is the only way to get this knowledge into your consciousness. What are the ritual elements in our practice? We'll answer these questions more fully during the coming weeks.

Promises Kept and Promises Broken

So, we have been promised the inheritance of the land. And we are having a problem with this promise. We are caught in a dilemma. Promises have been made before, and why should we be so quick to trust in promises? The following story is about just this very dilemma:

A traveler has been on the road for many years searching for his dream. He is weary and disillusioned. As he sits to rest at the side of the road, a man approaches him and says, over that mountain that you are now approaching there is a wonderful palace that is waiting for you. It is your palace and everything in it is yours. All you have to do is go there and claim it.

Now, our traveler has been on the road a long time and he has met many people along the way. He has been lied to. He has been cheated. He has had losses and many disappointments. And here is someone telling him that a wonderful palace is his and waiting for him. It is understandable that he may not believe this man. After all, why should he again be disappointed? And so we have a real Catch-22. He wants to realize his dream, but does not want to walk toward it, and he cannot realize his dream unless he walks toward it. What is the answer to this dilemma? You are this traveler. You have come here to learn meditation and many of you are seeking something that at best is elusive, namely self-realization. And here there is a teaching and a tradition that is saying it is attainable and is actually waiting for you to claim it. But you have had many experiences in life. You have been lied to. You have been betrayed by people you thought were close to you. You have had losses, both emotional and financial. You have had disappointments. How will you solve this dilemma?

The real question here is what will induce or inspire you to go to claim your palace, and the answer is that you must first know that it is there. Even if the rest of the story told to you is false, without the knowledge that there is, in fact, something there, you will not move toward it. So, here a compromise is necessary, and the compromise is this. You must set out on the journey toward the palace but a full commitment is not necessary. And so you need to travel just far enough to see a little bit of the palace. Now you know that it is there and that is enough for you to make the rest of the journey. The meditative experience is like that. Once experienced, the mind can no longer deny its existence. The rest is our choice.

There is, of course, an inherent assumption in the above story. Is it your goal to claim the palace that awaits you? The clarification of this question has to do with the definiteness of your purpose. And so we see that kavannah is one of the ingredients. Intent is the first step in developing the motivation necessary to persist on your journey.

I now have intent, but do I have a sincere desire to reach my destination? Is it, indeed, something that I want? You see, having a destination and wanting to be in that destination are different aspects. What is it that you want? Clarify this thought. Write it down and reflect on it for a few minutes daily. Embellish it. Refine its details. Rotate it in the mind.

No matter what has happened in the past, begin from this moment to believe in yourself. You have the ability to reach your destination. It is an inner journey of transforming your life; it is within the power of everyone to do this. Knowing this, remain steadfast in your determination. Persist and you will realize the benefits of your work.

Your Practice

At this time we'll continue our journey toward a meditative practice with a guided relaxation. Do this practice on either a mat or a carpeted floor. Lie on your back with your legs about twenty inches apart and the arms at the sides of the body, a few inches away from the body; the palms are turned upward, and the fingers are gently curled. The eyes are closed and the focus is inward.

Bring your awareness to your breath. Without sending the breath anywhere or directing its motion, speed or rhythm, simply observe the breath. Follow the breath with your mind. Observe how it moves in the body.

Allow your body to become heavier, to sink more fully into the supporting mat or carpet. All day long gravity is working to push us down toward the earth. What acts against this force? Why are we not crushed down? It is the muscles that resist this downward pressure. At this time do not resist the movement of gravity. On the contrary, let gravity work for you. Let yourself become heavier and heavier, to sink further into the supporting floor. Relaxation in a lying down position, therefore, means surrendering your body to gravity, just letting go.

Take a mental journey through the body, from the crown of the head to the tips of the toes. Systematically review each part of the body and if you discover tension anywhere, just let it go. With each breath, allow yourself to relax more deeply, to let go more completely. When you reach the tips of the toes, begin to move back upward through the body to the crown of the head.

Bring the awareness fully to the breath. Allow the breath to be smooth, gentle, deep and even. If any distractions arise, acknowledge them but try to let them go. Remain focused and centered within yourself. Continue with this practice of breath awareness and deepening relaxation within your own silence for 10 minutes.

After 10 minutes, bring awareness back to the body by gently moving the extremities. Move the fingers and toes; open and close the hands, move the feet. Bring your hands together and rub the hands briskly until the palms are warm. Cover the eyes with the palms and take a moment to let the warmth and darkness penetrate the eyelids. Open the eyes into the warmth and darkness of the palms, and, with the next inhalation, come into a long overhead stretch; bring the legs together. Stretch the toes and flex the toes. Bring the knees up into the chest. Take the knees with the hands and gently rock the knees in toward the chest, releasing any tension that may have built up in the lower back. Roll onto your left side, and when you're ready, come to an easy sitting position.

Sit up straight. Observe good posture. Take two or three sitting breaths and end your relaxation practice for this session. If you are doing this work in a group, ending the session with a group chant is a powerfully energizing and uplifting experience. You may use any chant from any tradition. The only caution I would offer is to use a universal chant rather than one which specifies deities or a specific religious orientation, unless you are in a closed group that shares the same religious ideas. Journal your experience.

The assignment for you is to develop your sitting practice for fifteen minutes a day and to continue with self-guided relaxation once a day. In both instances journal your experiences, and review your journal weekly. This is the process of self-examination and awakening of self-consciousness.

Why do we seek a guide through this landscape of the mind? What is the benefit of this? You have been on a particular road for some time and now you have set off on a new road. Or perhaps you have been on this very road but you are now coming to a new part of this road that you are not familiar with. Are there any pitfalls? Where are the cliffs? Can I travel this road by night, or do I need sunlight to light my way? A guide in this instance is someone who has traveled this very road and can tell you, "about one mile down the road you will come to a fork; at that fork turn right because of the deep pits to the left. Also, when you see the cliffs, take the path nearer to the sea. It appears longer, but will actually shorten your journey. "

This new road is not necessarily easier than the one you have been on. There will no doubt be setbacks. It is the nature of travel. If you go sailing, there will be calm waters with good winds, but there will also be times of rough waters. If your expectation is smooth sailing all the way, you may be unnecessarily disappointed.

Questions for Chapter IV

1. List different kinds of rituals.
2. What is the dictionary definition of "ritual," and is this a useful definition?
3. What is the meaning of the two terms, *niglah* and *nistar*?
4. What are the *niglah* and the *nistar* aspects of *tefillin*?
5. What is the great mantra of the Jewish faith? Explain its meaning.
6. What are the *niglah* and the *nistar* aspects of *mezuzah*?
7. What is a basic tenet in the esoteric traditions?
8. Discuss the concept of *kavannah*.
9. Name one core belief that blocks us from understanding the power of ritual.
10. Explain why a ritual would be invalid or ineffective if any of its steps is omitted or changed.
11. What is the purpose of ritual guidebook?
12. What circumstances have stopped our imaginary traveler from claiming his palace?

Chapter V
The Breath

I Am Already Breathing

We begin our session with a sitting practice as in our previous session. Observe the physical elements and the mental commitment to time and place. And then continue with the practice of breath awareness for 15 minutes.

Today's discussion will deal with what is perhaps the single most important topic in developing a meditative practice and for our physical and mental health in general. In fact, without this function, there is no physical and mental being as we know it. That function is the breath.

Now you may ask a very good question. Why do we need to discuss anything at all about the breath? After all, don't we all breathe? In fact, if we weren't breathing we wouldn't even be here to read this material or to participate in this program. On a simple level, this is very true. However, many of the great masters in the esoteric traditions have emphasized the importance, no, the absolutely essential nature of the breath in getting in touch with the deepest energies within us and in the universe.

Breath is one path to the real pranayama. Breath is the vehicle of prana as everything is the vehicle of prana.

Penetrating all of existence is akasa. It is that out of which the universe has evolved. It is akasa that becomes all the forms in the universe. It is akasa that is the air, the fire, the water, and the earth. It is akasa that is man and akasa that is a speck of dust. Yet, akasa does not have the power of generation. What is the power that generates akasa? It is prana.

Both akasa and prana are eternal, infinite. One is the eternal material and the other is the eternal and ever-present power of manifestation. All manifest in akasa and dissolves into akasa.

Prana is magnetism. Prana is revolution. Prana is gravity. Prana is the current that travels through the nadis, and the current that carries thought-forms. All manifestation is prana. All things returning to their first state are prana.

In the stillness before motion prana was there, and akasa. Then prana striking like a hammer on the anvil of akasa awakened motion and the universe was born.

The Senses Dispute among Themselves

There is an ancient Hindu story about a debate that was taking place between all the senses of man. Each was claiming that it is the most important. As the debate continued they were not able to agree which of them was indeed the most important. Then they hit upon the following plan. They decided that each of them would leave the body for one day and thus they would determine how the others fared. The sense that will be most sorely missed, they reasoned, would be considered the most important.

The first sense to leave was the sense of smell. As the day came to a close, the sense of smell returned and asked, "Well, how did you do without me?" The other senses responded that it was difficult, that food did not taste as good, that there was lessened pleasure without the usual aromas and fragrances; it was also observed that some of the bad smells were eliminated. And, in this manner they continued to converse among themselves.

Next, the sense of hearing left. After one day, the sense of hearing returned and asked the same question regarding its own absence. The other senses responded by saying that the sense of hearing was indeed missed, but they were able to manage. "Yes," they said, "it's true that we could not hear the beautiful music that we had enjoyed in the past; it is true that we could not participate in the wonderful discussions, but, nevertheless, we were able to manage." And some of the senses added, "We also did not hear a lot of the unpleasant noise that occasionally disturbs us."

Now, the sense of sight left. The other senses became quite disconcerted for a short while. And although it is the nature of impermanent things to find fault and some statements could be heard about not having to see the ugliness in the world, nevertheless, this was a much greater adjustment, they all agreed. When the sense of sight returned, the other senses almost gave the coveted prize of "most important" to it. But, they said, although the world had become an externally dark place, there was still some hope in the fact that the other senses became stronger and began to compensate for the loss of sight.

And so it went with the other two senses. But then, it came time for the breath to leave, and do you know what happened then? I think you know the answer. When the breath left, it was gone for just a few moments when the other senses all cried out, "Come back! Come back!" Therefore, and from then on, it was determined that the breath is the most important sense, and that without this sense, the others could not function.

What is the breath? Why, in fact, do we need to breathe at all? The breath is a vapor and a bubble. It is the air inhaled and expelled in the respiratory system. Breath is air in gentle motion (and sometimes not so gentle motion). And this air in gentle motion affects every organ and every body system; it connects the mind and the body. For all its apparent intangibility, breath is the vehicle of energy and it is that substance that is the necessary ingredient for the transformation of nutrients into energy.

The breath is both individual and universal. Everything

in creation follows an ebb and a flow. The Universe is said to be an exhalation of God's breath, and when God begins to inhale the whole of creation will once again be drawn toward one point. This is the concept of the cosmic breath.

The Koshas

A good understanding of the position of the breath in "the scheme of things" may be gotten from the yogic model of sheaths. In Yoga philosophy we find that existence manifests in a series of *koshas*, or sheaths. Tradition teaches that there are five such *koshas*; these may be visualized as circles within circles. The five *koshas*, respectively from the outside in, are

Anna-maya-kosha	the physical
Prana-maya-kosha	the breath
Mano-maya-kosha	the mind
Vijnana-maya-kosha	the intellect
Ananda-maya-kosha	bliss

The English correspondences are familiar, but for our work exact definitions may be more useful. Thus, the physical refers to the body, and "body" is the frame or material organized substance of a thing in distinction from the vital principle, or that part we refer to as soul or spirit.

For breath, the simplest definition is the air inhaled and exhaled in the act of respiration. However, some of the more subtle definitions of "breath" apply to our model, namely, to inspire, to live, to rest from action, to emanate, to infuse and to send out.

Mind refers to those aspects that we call thought and intention.

The word *maya* means temporal. *Kosha*, we have seen, means sheath. A *maya-knosha*, therefore, may be said to be a temporal sheath, a vessel or a vehicle for the particular body being transported. The body, in this case, is actually three in number, and each of these is transported by a specific maya-kosha.

The three bodies are the physical body, the astral body, and the causal body. The physical body is carried by both anna-maya-kosha and prana-maya-kosha; the astral body is carried by mano-maya-kosha and vijnana-maya-kosha; and the causal body is carried by ananda-maya-kosha. The koshas, maya, and the three bodies together represent expressions of consciousness.

Prana, although associated with the breath, is not the breath. It is the primal energy in the universe, and breath is its finest vehicle. Equivalent terms exist in various cultures for this concept. In English we refer to Spirit. In Latin, the word is Spiritus. In the Greek, it is Pneuma. In the Chinese culture, it is called Qi or Chi. In the Kabbalistic tradition, the word is Ruakh. A full discussion of this subject is outside the parameters of the present work.

For our purposes, we are only interested at this time in three of these koshas, namely, anna-maya-kosha, prana-maya-kosha, and mano-maya-kosha – the physical, the breath, and the mind. These together represent the physical body and part of the astral body. Thus, we see that the breath is the sheath between the physical level and the mental level. We'll refer to the physical as the body and the mental level as mind for easier understanding. The breath, then, is said to be a bridge between the mind and the body, ***and the breath has an impact on both.***

The Body-Breath-Mind
Connection

The ancient masters in many traditions studied the breath closely. Today, with the advent of science and scientific method, many of the occult teachings are held in low esteem, and it is all too easy to make the mistake of understanding these early masters in the light of current history. However, these were not flighty individuals. On the contrary, they were the finest minds of their time, they were the deepest thinkers and most observant of scientists. They were the astronomers and chemists of their day; they were the philosophers and mathematicians of their day; they were keen observers of nature and of man, and as they studied the breath they observed an interesting phenomenon.

They observed that when an individual was physically injured or ill, there were changes in the rate of respiration. And they observed further that individuals in emotional distress also exhibited changes in respiration. Therefore, they reasoned that the body and the mind both affect the breath. Anyone with any experience of these matters can confirm these observations. I spent some years as an emergency medical technician on a neighborhood volunteer ambulance service. This experience of seeing people in all stages of physical trauma has made it easy for me to understand the observations of these masters so many thousands of years ago. The human condition has not changed so radically in this short period of time. The consciousness and awareness of an individual living four thousand years ago is not substantially different from the consciousness of modern man. Visit an emergency room sometime and sit there for a brief time, and you too will observe what these ancient masters observed.

What is amazing is the tremendous leap of the mind that they made from this observation to the intuitive reasoning that said, "if the mind and body affect the breath, *what if we became the masters of the breath? Could we then, not affect the mind and body?*" And, of course, they were perfectly correct. Their realization and teaching is part of our current knowledge and practice.

When a woman gets pregnant and goes for classes in childbirth, what is it that she is taught? She is taught to breath in a specific way. Many pain management clinics throughout the United States today teach breath-work to manage pain. Yes, they also provide pharmaceutical drugs and other therapies, but they include breath-work as part of the overall strategy for management and recovery. It is not an exaggeration to state that every condition of the body and mind can respond favorably or unfavorably to certain breathing patterns.

People in theater have long recognized that breathing can alleviate stage fright, and gentle, slow breathing has generally been found to be relaxing for the body and mind. My masters have taught me that *for every condition of the body or mind there is a corresponding breathing pattern.* This idea is pivotal in our understanding of the importance of the breath. As we change the pattern of our breath we have the power to change physical and mental patterns. All the great masters were masters of the breath, and this power was one of the great secrets of their apparent superhuman abilities.

In the Kabbalistic tradition there are numerous references to the relationship between the breath and spirituality. Insights into this relationship are given through the gematria, the numerological system that is the 29th principle of exegesis. A rudimentary knowledge of the Hebrew letters and their numerical equivalencies is required to understand these correspondences. However, a simple example may suffice. The word for air in Hebrew is composed of the letters alef, vav, yod and reysh. If we remove the letter vav, we actually have the spelling of the word air. Changing the order of these letters and adding the letter that signifies God, we find the word is composed of the letters yod, reysh, alef and heh. This word signifies *fear* of God in the sense of awe, and in scripture we discover that the beginning of wisdom is "fear" of God, or awe as our inner perception awakens to the true scope of creation.

The Hebrew letters of the word AIR represent respectively the Torah, the commandments and the path of life. The meaning is clear: to live by the Torah, to follow the commandments, is to be on the path of life. If the order of the words is rearranged we discover the word YRA, yod, reysh, alef, and this word signifies the "fear" of Heaven. Adding the letter hey the word becomes YRAH; the hey is symbolic of the realization of the world, and this word is the "fear" of God. Rearranging the letters of YRAH we get RAYH and this word means "lung." It is through the lungs that we receive life.

A Brief Physiology of Breath

Is there a correct way of breathing? To answer this question, it is necessary to understand the physiology of breath. This is certainly not a course on anatomy and physiology, so we will limit our discussion to those elements that will shed light on the subject of correct breathing.

Breathing is part of the cardio-respiratory process. This is a circular process and it is called the circulatory system. This process begins with the inspiration of oxygen from the surrounding atmosphere. We breathe in through the nose or through the mouth, preferably the nose, and the air travels through the larynx (the voice box) to the trachea (the windpipe). The trachea then branches off into the bronchi, and the air then moves down into the lungs.

At the bottom of the lungs are air sacs called alveoli and it is here that the oxygen is picked up and delivered to the heart. The oxygen is then pumped out by the left side of the heart, through the arterial system (the arteries), to each and every cell of the body to provide energy for the entire organism. The blood traveling through the arteries is oxygen-rich blood and this is the reason that when an artery is cut, the blood is seen to be a bright red in color.

This oxygen-rich blood is delivered to the 100 trillion cells of the body and used by these cells to convert carbohydrates and fats into usable energy. Carbon dioxide is the by-product of this process, and it is carbon dioxide that the body expires.

Carbon dioxide is picked up by the venous system (the veins) and transported back to the heart, and from the heart to the lungs, at which point we exhale. This blood carries the impurities that we rid ourselves of in the act of respiration. It is because of this that the venous blood is dark blood.

Breath is a process that is both voluntary and involuntary, and it is this fact that allows us to work with the breath consciously. The involuntary aspect of the breath is that it is regulated by the medulla oblongata of the brain. This automatic regulation usually accounts for 10-15 breaths per minute. A message is sent from the respiratory center of the brain to the diaphragm and to the rib muscles. They, in turn, contract and pull the lower surfaces of the lungs downward so that they may fill with air. The next message sent back to the brain is from the stretch receptors in the lungs, and this message causes the diaphragm and rib muscles to relax. The diaphragm then moves upward, returning to a flattened state, and the air is expired.

The infant is born and the first breath is taken. Before this first breath, life is of a different reality. The world of the unborn child is the controlled environment in which all is provided by the body fluids, the tissues and the bones of the mother; there is no direct relationship between the child and the external creation. This relationship is fully established with the baby's first breath.

Is this the first breath of life or the first breath of death? All things inherently contain their opposite. Thus, life contains within it the truth of its opposite. Yogic and Taoist teaching on this subject is that stopping the breath (holding the breath) and the practice of taking less breaths per minute are two techniques for prolonging life. It is taught that we come into the world with a certain amount of allotted breaths. When we use these breaths up, life ends. Therefore, the yogic masters of pranayama practice minimizing the amount of breaths taken per minute. Stopping the breath is a technique that must be learned with a teacher.

Types of Breath

Yoga science recognizes three types of breathing. First, thoracic breathing, that is, breathing into the chest; second, abdominal breathing in which the abdominal area expands with the breath; and, third, diaphragmatic breathing in which the diaphragm is utilized. Now, from what we have said previously about the breathing process, we may rightly ask, "Isn't the diaphragm naturally used in the automatic act of breathing?" The answer is that if we are breathing correctly, then the diaphragm is indeed used; however, many people have developed poor breathing habits and are not breathing correctly.

Let's find out what kind of breather you are. Sit up straight, either in a chair or on the floor. Place one hand over the navel area and the other hand over the center of the chest, and just take several breaths. Now determine where you had the most movement. If you had more movement in the chest, then you are probably a thoracic breather. If, on the other hand, you had more movement in the abdominal area, you may be either an abdominal or a diaphragmatic breather. So, let's go to step number two. For those of you that had more movement in the abdominal area, please place one hand over the navel and the other hand over the kidney area, and once again take several breaths. Now, here is the question. Did you feel any movement in the kidney area? If the answer is yes, than you may indeed be a diaphragmatic breather; however, if the answer is no then chances are pretty good that you are an abdominal breather.

Diaphragmatic breathing is desirous on every level. It is indeed the most efficient way of breathing, providing the maximum energy for the least effort. So, having determined your breathing type, for those of you who are not breathing correctly, how are we to correct the breath? I'm going to suggest a simple exercise and if you will practice this daily, your breathing style and pattern will improve and change.

At this time lie down on your back; if it makes you more comfortable, you may place a small pillow under the head for support. Have the legs about twenty inches apart as in our relaxation posture. Now place one hand over the navel area and the other over the center of the chest. In this position, unless you are doing something extremely unusual to force the breath into unnatural pathways, the body will naturally begin to breath diaphragmatically. Take ten breaths in this position observing closely the feeling of this process.

And now roll over unto your stomach. Place the right cheek on the floor (this is arbitrary for this experiment – it could be the left cheek), and just focus on the breath. You will observe that in this position, the abdomen and the chest are relatively immobile; the floor is stopping them from moving. So we might ask, are we breathing? Of course we are. So, where is the breath going? Place your hands over the kidney area and continue to breathe. Again, unless you are forcing the breath to do something other than what it naturally will do in this position, you are now feeling an expansion of that part of the lower back around the kidneys.

Now come to a sitting position, and let's try the experiment once again. Place one hand over the navel, the other over the kidney and just breathe. Use the following picture to help you with this practice. Diaphragmatic breathing does not fill the abdominal area only; it fills the entire center of the torso. This is called the "circle of air." Think of a bucket that is being filled with water. The bucket is not two-dimensional; it is three-dimensional and the entire bottom of the bucket is filling – the front, the sides, the back. Your torso is sort of like that bucket, and the air is like the water.

This is the real Da Tien of the Chinese. It is not the navel. It is the entire circle of air. There are two great forces in this system. There is Qi and there is Jing. Qi is the energy associated with all movement; it is the inherent energy within the movement. Jing is the substance that moves slowly in the process of change. Qi is the external, the yang, aspect of movement, while Jing is the darker yin, the inner essence of growth and decline. And so we discover in the Chinese system that the life force, that out of which Qi emerges, is in the kidneys. The kidneys are the storehouse of Jing, and Jing is the substance of life itself. When a boxer punches, where does his strength come from? It is certainly not his arm alone. It comes from the back of his hip as he puts his body into the punch. When a martial artist kicks, where is the power of the kick? But what is in the hip? What is in the arm? It is Qi. It is Prana. It is Ruakh.

Breath is the vehicle of this primal energy. It is the energy around which the physical body takes form. In the Tao Tsang, a Book on Breath by the Master Great Nothing of Sung-shan, the teacher writes,

"...the bodily form depends on the breath and... breath relies on form. When the breath is perfect, the form is perfect. If breath is exhausted, then form dies."

What is of interest is not only that form relies on breath, but that breath relies on form. What is this relationship? Just as form (the physical body) takes shape around a more subtle energy, so also does energy require a form in order to be actualized. What is an ocean without the boundaries of the basin in which it sits?

Perfect this relationship between breath and form before the need arises to do so. In a book on immortality, the Hsien Ching, it says that we treasure life when confronted by death, we appreciate justice and goodness after a crime has been committed, and we seek medical intervention when suffering and illness come into our lives.

The question is asked regarding wisdom. What is this quality? One definition of wisdom is to see the end of a thing from its beginning. It is to recognize causal relationships and ratio-relationships. It is the way of the wise to appreciate life before facing death. It is to be joyous. It is the way of the wise to walk in the paths of justice and goodness before the crime has been committed. And it is the way of the wise to treasure the breath and to prolong life before the need to seek medicines.

Here is a little homework. Each morning, after finishing your morning hygienic practice, and before starting the rest of your day, lie down on the floor just as we have done here and take ten breaths on your back and ten breaths on your stomach. The worst thing that will happen to you is that you will begin your day with twenty really good diaphragmatic breaths. The best thing that will happen is that your body will begin to remember the feeling of diaphragmatic breathing and will begin to duplicate it automatically. This aspect of the body is called "sense-memory," and it is, in fact, how we learn an entire range of automatic behaviors (i.e., driving a car, walking).

Finding my Master

A good number of years ago, when I was completing my formal studies in theology, I needed to make money to get through school, and I was fortunate in having some gift toward music. And so I went to work as a guitarist and lead singer with bands; we performed at all types of functions. Like many singers, I went for training with vocal coaches and vocal teachers. I was a tenor, and I was told that a tenor pulls his tones down from the top of the head, and that the tones bounce and are supported on the stream of air; then the mouth is shaped into an inverted megaphone for better projection, the abdominal muscles are tightened down for greater internal control, and so we sing; and you know, I actually followed these silly directions for several years. During this time, I began to truly not enjoy singing. Then, one day, while attending an advanced repertoire workshop with a great singer and teacher named Sidor Belarsky, he asked me to stay after the workshop and he said to me,

"You know, David, you are not a bad singer, but there is something wrong with the way you sing. I believe you could be much better than you are. Why don't you go and see a vocal teacher that I will recommend. Tell him that I have sent you and have suggested that you study with him." The teacher that he sent me to was Boris Belastosky, a Russian man whose studio was in the Ansonia Hotel in Manhattan.

I followed Sidor Belarsky's instructions and went to the Ansonia. When I first met Boris Belastosky, he asked me to sing a particular selection; he began to play the piano and I began to sing; I believe the selection was an Italian aria, Amarilli. After just one verse, he stopped me and asked me what it was that I was doing. And I explained,

"Well," I said, "I am tightening down on my abdominal muscles, bringing up a stream of air; then, I am pulling my tone down from the top of my head, and I am projecting my tone through my inverted megaphone."

Well, he looked at me as if I had just landed on earth from another planet. After a moment's silence, which, in hindsight, I now interpret as possibly disbelief, he said to me,

"This is what we are going to do from now on. I will play, and you will sing. When you are singing correctly, I will tell you that you are singing correctly, and when you are not singing correctly, I will stop you and tell you that you are not singing correctly. The only thing that I want you to do is to remember what it feels like to sing correctly, and to duplicate this feeling."

My teacher taught me many secrets with the simplicity of this way. I learned the concept of breathing carefully and of not dissipating my breath or my life-force by useless talking. Speak to purpose. When you sing, my teacher would say, each sound has significance. Let every sound, every note, travel together with emotional content. Avoid shouting. It damages the throat and wastes the breath. These simple things were very different from the artificial postures I had learned previously. I began to recognize that my breath was, in fact, in disarray and that the viscera and the receptacles were not in harmony. When the form and the breath are in harmony, knowledge of the soul awakens.

Sense-Memory

I remained with Boris Belastosky for several years. He was, he is my teacher, and with him I became a somewhat decent singer. Over these years, I discovered that he had been one of an inner circle of students that worked with Stanislavsky and so I learned about sense-memory. Remember, there are two traditions by which we learn: one is the scholastic tradition, that is, the imparting and receiving of information; the other is the monastic, or experiential tradition. You have sufficient scholastic knowledge from our discussion to understand the breathing process and the breathing mechanisms, but this information by itself will not help you to breath correctly. By doing the simple exercise I have given you here, I am passing on what my teacher has given to me.

We have offered two positions in which to experience correct breathing. However, simple exercise in different positions, or assuming different postures in the yogic tradition, or, for that matter, simply assuming certain body positions, it becomes immediately evident that the body wants to breath correctly. You can try this for yourself by squatting, or crouching over. If you are familiar with Yogic postures, you might try the child or the crocodile.

Remember what it feels like to breath diaphragmatically, and at different times throughout the day try to duplicate the feeling. Let your body teach you. If we have developed a faulty breathing habit, we can also change this habit by replacing it with proper breathing.

For every birth there is a death. To breathe properly, incorrect breathing habits have to be discarded. To have a higher vision, a lower needs to die. It is the principle of growth and development throughout the universe.

Certainly avoid focusing on the breath excessively as you practice correct breathing. This exercise is not about becoming stressed or focusing on how to breath each moment of the day; but every now and then, when you are taking a break at work, or sitting on the subway, or walking, remind yourself and take a few correct breaths. The body will begin to remember and you will correct the breathing. In the course of time, breath awareness and correct breathing will be established.

Trust your subconscious to learn what it needs to learn. Guide it with your conscious mind, but allow it to do the work that it knows how to do quite well. We are constantly receiving sensations and these sensations become a part of our past experience. Experience, in turn, becomes a part of our conscious and subconscious memory. Somewhere between these two levels of mind, conclusions are drawn, but they occur within the deductive stream of the subconscious mind. We have experienced a sensation and somehow interpreted this experience, and it is this interpretation that has become the working thesis from which a complex structure is erected.

It would be simple to bring about change by "changing our thesis," our working principle, but things are not as simple as they appear. Our memory is not only an accumulation of our past experiences within our lifetime. There is the idea of a collective unconscious postulated by Carl Jung. There are theories of genetic memory. Some philosophers have spoken about cellular memory; this type of memory would connect us to all other cellular life since the beginning of cellular life in the universe – the reason being that all cells are fundamentally the same. If we continue along these lines, we may say that even cells have molecular and subatomic structure. Therefore, are we not one with the very fabric of the Universe and *is our memory not a part of that fabric?* It is at these, and all other levels, that we may experience the universal process of expansion and contraction that is said to be the cosmic breath.

We've said that there is a close relationship between breath and mind and that each influences the other. This is obvious in cases where strong emotion has overcome one's equilibrium. And further, if we create certain breathing patterns, corresponding mental patterns may be stimulated into manifestations. The mechanical parts of breathing continue with or without our involvement, but the breath may be controlled by the mind. The mind is a more subtle level than the breath. If the mind is distracted and unruly, the breath also will be disordered.

Consider this principle of order. We live in an ordered Universe. All scientists agree, whether they acknowledge a higher power or not, that the Universe has an "intelligent" structure. It is the concept of the "isotropic" universe. The only question that has been debated is whether intelligence and order emerges out of chaos or whether intelligence is the precedent of this process and we move toward greater chaos toward eventual dissolution. It is the debate whether spirit preceded matter or matter preceded spirit. Scientists, philosophers, and theologians have had this conversation for several thousand years.

It is again a problem of perception. We say there is order in the Universe, but is the order inherent in the Universe or inherent in our perception of the Universe. Here again is the problem of the observed and the observer. Is the idea of an ordered universe, in fact, absolutely important or only relatively important? If I sing a song there is a melody of individual notes moving across space and time. It is a temporal reality. But how are we to understand reality that is not temporal? It is our need to establish a reality consistent with our perceptual limitations that is the very reality we change in a meditative state.

Your Practice

We'll conclude our session with sitting meditation on the breath, and next week we will look at the concepts of mantra and yantra, and begin to incorporate the use of mantra meditation.

At this time, observe the physical elements and the mental commitment of your practice. Continue with the practice of breath awareness at the point between the upper lip and the nostrils for twenty minutes.

If you are doing this work in a group, ending the session with a group chant is a powerfully energizing and uplifting experience. You may use any chant from any tradition. The only caution I would offer is to use a universal chant rather than one which specifies deities or a specific religious orientation, unless you are in a closed group that shares the same religious ideas.

During the coming week continue to incorporate a relaxation practice and a twenty minute sitting practice of breath awareness.

Questions for Chapter V

1. Which of the senses is most important, and how was this determined?
2. What is the breath?
3. Explain the cosmic breath.
4. Name and draw a schematic of the five *koshas*.
5. Give the exact definitions of the three outermost *koshas*.
6. What is *maya*? What is *kosha*? Explain *maya-kosha*.
7. What are the three bodies transported by the *koshas*?
8. Which *koshas* transport which bodies?
9. In what way is the breath strategically placed in the first three *koshas*, and what is the significance of this placement?
10. Explain the power of the breath.
11. What is the relationship of breath to the circulatory system? Explain in detail.
12. Explain the involuntary aspect of the breath.
13. What are the three types of breathing categorized by the yogic system?
14. Explain the concept of sense-memory.

Chapter VI
Practical Aspects

Established in Mantra

We begin our session with a sitting practice as in our previous session. Observe the physical elements and the mental commitment. Today, we will add the use of a mantra. There are, of course, many mantras. The one that we will use is a universal mantra that has been used by millions of initiates and adepts alike. That mantra is So...Hum, repeating mentally the sound So... with inspiration, and the sound Hum... with the expiration. Establish your sitting position, close the eyes and take one minute to focus the mind on the breath. And then continue with the practice of breath awareness with the repetition of the mantra. Throughout the practice, remain with this focus. If you observe that the mind has wandered or been distracted by other thoughts or external stimuli, bring your focus gently back to mantra. Continue with this practice for twenty minutes. Then release the focus on the sound of the mantra, bring the awareness back to the breath, and from the breath to the sitting position of the body. Now gently open the eyes.

We've discussed physiological, psychological and metaphysical aspects of the meditative tradition. A recurring question is the scientific validity of these teachings. What is the scientific approach? Something is observed, a principle is postulated, and, after the principle is tested in a repeated set of circumstances, knowledge is gained. Specific knowledge is always theoretic in the world of science because a new theory may come about to supplant the one we currently hold. It is this awareness of the temporal nature of our knowledge that is the inherent principle of humility within the scientific community.

If we are to postulate a theorem and prove it by experience and experiment then we must follow the steps necessary to bring about the result we have postulated.

In today's talk I want to address very practical aspects of meditation. You are here because you want to develop a meditative practice. In order to do that we will look at the "ritual" elements involved in developing such a practice.

Trip-Planning

In every endeavor in life, some preparation is necessary. If we want to take a trip from New York City to Los Angeles, California, we would no doubt route our trip with maps and timetables; we would decide the nature of the trip. Is it a vacation? Is it a business trip? Based on its nature, we would then prepare what we need to take along. If our preparations have been carried out, and barring any unseen obstacles (and there usually are a few), we will reach our destination and the experience will be a positive experience. Any other example may be used and I'm quite sure you can think of many examples of your own. So, here's the question.

If we believe, if we know, that the success of any project in the physical realm requires considerable preparation, why is it that so many individuals believe that work in the spiritual or mental realm requires less? On the contrary, the work of the spirit requires more preparation than the work of the body. And, thus, the first level of preparation is very appropriately the body.

Is this confusing? The Rambam, Maimonides, said that it is difficult for a person to pray to God or focus on the spiritual dimension when he or she is in a state of physical disease. The body is a great distraction and it takes a very exceptional individual to overcome the pain and discomfort of the body, and still maintain a meditative and spiritual practice. There are, of course, genetic factors that influence the state of our physical and mental health, and these are beyond our control. There are trials and challenges that are placed before us in order for us to learn what we need to learn in our present incarnation. Fortunately, most conditions of health and disease are environmentally produced and, therefore, within our control. What do I mean by "environmentally" produced? Anything that is not inherent within us, anything that is not genetically determined, is coming from the environment. This includes all our life-style choices: our food, our air, our water, our clothes, our exercise and hygiene habits, our relationships, our mental and emotional choices and so on.

We can take this idea of health even further. The mind is the most powerful thing we have and it is within the power of the mind to change physiological and psychological states. I am not advocating that when a physical condition exists you try to overcome it with the mind alone. Certainly, at the very minimum, a good diagnosis is required by a qualified health care worker to determine the nature of the problem. And modern medicine, for all its shortcomings, has come a long way in dealing with some conditions. However, the latest and most cutting-edge field of medical intervention is the field of *psycho-neuroimmunology*, in which there is the recognition of the pivotal role that is played by the mind in both disease and recovery, and the relationship of mental patterns to the state of our immune system. One of our life-style choices is how we take care of the mind and body.

What is the nature of this relationship? Something is perceived and we respond to that perception. But that does not give us a lot of information. Why do we respond as we do to a perception? In this case, scientists speak about the construct of the personality. But this construct itself is based on a foundation. It itself is not the cause, but the result of some deeper principle. In fact, the laws of cause and effect may not be applicable because the further in we search, the more we discover cause behind cause behind cause ad infinitum. This is not to say that there are not immediate causes of events, but these causes are themselves the results of previous causes.

Subjective reality is formed from a substratum that, at best, we term *homo-sapiens*, on which we construct human personality. From this subjective world, we observe and interpret the so-called objective world. It is little wonder that "liberation" is a difficult state to achieve. In order to discover freedom, we must peel away layers of "objective" reality, of constructs, of subjective reality, and beyond these, the archetypes, and past the archetypes to the very foundations of our "human" nature. Some have referred to this point beyond foundation as the One Mind; others call this God. Many teachings have appeared to mystify the subject. This may be because the subject does not lend itself well to expression through language. And so we focus on method and approach.

This approach to living recognizes the distinction between exogenous and endogenous factors. Genetics are endogenous and we may not be able to do much about this. With the advances in research in the field of genetics, endogenous factors may indeed become an area of choice rather than compulsion. However, the exogenous factors are mainly under our control and within our power to choose. It is interesting to note that this balance is somehow changing and that which we considered endogenous may come into our realm of control, whereas many of the exogenous factors, especially those of environment such as air quality, water quality, noise pollution, sanitation in our inner cities, and so on, may be less and less within our control and ability to choose.

It is in the mundane, repetitious acts requiring self-discipline that we discover some of our greatest strengths and our greatest weaknesses. The glamorous and romantic is always easier for us to commit to doing. Why is that? The answer is simple. It is exactly because it is glamorous and romantic. There is no romance in persisting, but there is also no substitute for this quality.

We are challenged, and we need to make good choices between the various alternatives in exogenous factors. What should these choices be?

Taking Care of the Body

What are the elements of taking care of the body? Well, personal hygiene is certainly one of the critical elements. Take a shower every day – hot to cold to stimulate the circulation; wash your hair as often as needed (oily hair daily, medium hair three or four times weekly, dry hair twice weekly); brush your teeth (don't forget to floss); skin brush (a good practice for stimulating the circulation and cleansing the skin of dead cells).

More esoteric hygienic practices are also available, such as yogic neti pot, internal washes (upper wash, stomach wash, colon wash) If any of the latter interest you, they should be pursued under the guidance of a teacher.

One of my teachers, Bernard Jensen, used to say that autointoxication is the number one source of all the misery and decay we find in society and culture today. It is by this internal uncleanness that we develop imbalance, sickness and disease. Good hygienic practices are the path to outward and inward physical cleanliness.

Food for the Body is Food for the Mind

What about food? Is this important? Oh, I don't mean just any food. Is the quality and quantity of food that you consume significant in developing a good meditative practice? Clearly, the quality and quantity of food that you put into your body has repercussions on every part of your life. If the body is undernourished or malnourished, if the body develops chronic or temporary pains and discomforts, if the body develops serious illness, it becomes very difficult to sit in meditation. In fact, although meditation may help the situation, it is difficult to focus the mind under such conditions, and the disease conditions themselves demand our attention and become our priorities.

So what is good food? How are we to choose? Do we need to go to a nutritionist or a dietician? Well, these are not bad options if we want to have an in-depth evaluation and a streamlined, customized nutritional program. However, there are some relatively simple steps that we can take and principles that we can follow which can simply transform our lives.

To understand the principles, we need to know from where we have come. We have come from the earth. Now, I'm not speaking of the soul. That comes from a different source. But our bodies and everything that makes up our bodies comes from the earth. Each part of our body is predominantly made up of a different mineral. Our bones are calcium structures; our blood is an iron-based system; our stomach lining is sodium; our thyroid is iodine. These are the minerals needed to maintain and strengthen these parts of our body. From where will we get these minerals?

The answer is obvious. Minerals are in the earth, and somehow we need to get them from the earth into our bodies. We are not going to consume them in their pure, isolated form as they exist in rocks and earth. We are going to get them from the plant or the animal kingdoms as they are transformed through the metabolism of these life forms into a form suitable for our consumption. Many esoteric traditions suggest a vegetarian life-style as being more conducive for meditation. This needs to be a personal choice. Many people do quite well on a vegetarian diet, but there are individuals for which this type of diet may not be suitable. Whatever your choice, the following considerations will improve your overall health and well-being.

Here is the principle then: *The closer a food is to the earth, the more life it has to give you.*" And the corollary of that is "*the further a food is from the earth, the less life it has to give you.*" These statements refer to the processing of food. Thus, canned fruits and vegetables have absolutely zero nutrient value for your body. Frozen fruits and vegetables have approximately 40% food value; and fresh fruits and vegetables have approximately 60-85% food value, depending on the soils and how far from ripening they are picked.

Nuts and seeds are relatively close to the earth, but not when they are roasted and/or salted. Legumes are close to the earth, but not when they are canned. Canned beans, however, do retain their protein. Protein is not as affected by processing.

What about grains? Well, grains need to have all the elements that give life; they need to contain all the B vitamins, the vitamin E (in the wheat germ), the octacosanol, the fiber (in the bran), and all these and more are available in the whole grain. Once processed into white flour or white sugar, all the positive elements have been removed; isolated forms of these elements are put back in, and we refer to these foods as fortified. Don't be fooled. Eat the real thing.

Dairy products! I have a real problem with this food, and therefore, a problem in recommending it. It is not a case of dairy being bad for you. Unless you come from a cultural background or have a personal history in which lactose is a problem for your digestion, I can only point out that entire civilizations have arisen and thrived around a dairy-based diet. But, unfortunately, the dairy that we are eating today is not the same dairy that did indeed lead to the rise of certain societies. For thousands of years, much of the human race thrived on dairy products. I remember as a child going with my grandmother to the local farmer to get fresh bottled milk that had come from his cows just that morning. She would bring the milk home and when she would serve it, she put it into a pot, brought it to one swift boil, and it was ready.

What is the procedure for processing dairy products today? They are pasteurized and this means that they are cooked at high temperatures thousands of times. Anything that might be of value in dairy is burned out. Certainly the lecithin is destroyed leaving a cholesterol-heavy food. Additionally, we have become the guinea pigs for a grand experiment in carcinogenic additives in the feed provided to our cattle. They are given *bovine growth hormone* in order to produce more milk; this is economically productive, but bovine growth hormone has been shown to cause mastitis, a precursor of breast cancer, in over 50% of test animals.

So, what are the choices? If you are going to have dairy products, buy organic. It is readily available today in many supermarkets and the prices have come down dramatically. As for cheeses, buy organic, raw cheese.

What about other sources of protein? There is meat, fowl and fish. For meat eaters, each of these has benefits and drawbacks. The subject is outside the parameters of the present work, but there are many well-written books on nutrition. Don't be fooled by the latest fads in diet. Stay with basics. Keep your eating simple and follow the dictates of common sense. In most cases you will do just fine.

Physical Exercise for Mental Focus

Another building block in the structure that we are erecting is exercise. There is no replacement for exercise. Our bodies were meant to be in motion. We come from a lineage of hunter/gatherers, a people whose physical prowess would have given our best athletes pause. In fact, it is doubtful that our best athletes could have competed with any of these early people in strength, speed or endurance. What kind of exercise do you need?

Well, every exercise program needs to be individualized, but basically you need to have five elements in order to be fit: first, a good heart and lungs and that requires aerobic, and sometimes anaerobic, exercise. Some aerobic exercises are swimming, walking, hiking, bicycling and jogging – what is meant by aerobic exercise is any exercise that is continuous, that raises the heart rate to a "target" rate, and that keeps the heart at its target rate for a set period of time (usually 30-45 minutes). Second, muscular strength; we need to know that our leg muscles, for example, will take us across a room; we need to know that we can carry a baby around during postpartum. Third, muscular endurance; so, you can walk across a room, but how far can you walk before your leg muscles give out? A certain level of muscular endurance is a pre-requisite for fitness. Fourth, we need flexibility. Stretching daily will go a long way in keeping the body youthful and generally more vibrant. And fifth, muscle to fat ratio. We certainly want more muscle than fat on the body.

How do we determine our fitness in these areas? What are the definitions that we need in order to correctly evaluate our status? Cardio-respiratory, also called the cardio-vascular system refers to three functional components of the human body, namely, cardiac function (the heart), respiratory function (the lungs), and arterial and venous circulation (the blood vessels). Muscular strength refers to the amount of force your muscles can develop during a contraction (i.e., how much can you lift?). Muscular endurance refers to how long or how many repetitions a muscle or muscle group can perform against a given resistance before becoming fatigued (i.e., once you've lifted the weight, how long can you hold it up?). Flexibility is the amount of movement at a joint; this is called the joint articulation; we generally refer to this as "the range of motion." Body to fat ratio addresses the issue of body composition. Our body is composed of two types of weight. First, there is body fat made up of adipose tissue; and, second, there is fat-free weight made up of muscle and bone as well as the liquids in our body (water, blood, lymph, digestive juices) and the organs.

In developing your own fitness program do some research. Read one or two books, explore some of the gyms in your area, talk to fitness trainers, talk to friends who are knowledgeable about fitness training, or simply develop a lifestyle that includes good outdoor activity. There are many ways. Find something you enjoy doing that will keep your body fit, and do it.

What about weights, or resistance training? Yes, these are also good, but we don't need weights to do resistance training

– push-ups, chins, dips, are all very effective exercises utilizing one's own body-weight as resistance. There are so many gyms available today. If you feel uncomfortable about creating your own exercise program, take a short membership in a local gym, and let a personal trainer create a program for you. However you pursue this, learn to listen closely to your body. It is lack of attention that causes injury. Set your ego aside during exercise and spend more time listening to your body; it will tell you its capacity and this will protect you from injury. Of course, challenging the body to its comfortable extreme is necessary for progress; remember that phrase, "comfortable extreme."

We each have an image of ourselves. Often this image is distorted. Someone who was once obese may see himself as obese even if he has lost the weight and is now quite fit. It may take some time to transform this inner image, and yet that is exactly what we must do. As we follow the steps necessary for fitness and physical well-being, our inner perception of self begins to change around the new mental patterns we are creating. It is true that the meditative journey will take us beyond these aspects of self, beyond the constructs of ego or self-image; yet, in order to persist along this journey, this image of self must have the power to carry us forward through the struggles and challenges that arise along the way.

Be good to yourself. Nourish your self with the best of nutrients. Appreciate your gifts. Learn to like yourself and trust in your ability to see things through. It is an interesting phenomenon that most of us think less of ourselves than is actually warranted. We look into our own hearts and our own memories and we discover there those truths that we have not shared with others. We discover the lies, the jealousies, the anger, the little theft, the disrespect, the cruelty and the pettiness. We see in ourselves the worst qualities of our species, and even when we balance these with our best qualities, there is within many of us the doubt that we are perhaps not deserving of the best things that life has to offer.

Truth is not simple. Yet, we take partial truths and give

them tremendous power over us. We build worlds around each small truth until there is within us an infrastructure that guides us in all that we do. Do not accept partial truths. Examine yourself fairly. One of the greatest tools of certain types of meditation (i.e., Kabbalah) is the imagination. Visual images, yantras, have a powerful influence on the mind. Learn to use these visual images to dwell in "the house of the Lord." That is, to dwell in joy and abundance, and in a more complete Truth.

Enjoy Yourself

Taking care of the body also involves spending some recreational time. *Do things you enjoy.* Go to a movie with a friend or your husband or wife. Go to a ballet, a concert, an art exhibit, go to the theater...Recreation and rest time begin to cross over between the body and mind. Friendship itself has a healing quality. It is written in Pirkei Avot, the Wisdom of the Fathers, that we are to find ourselves a teacher and *buy ourselves a friend.*

At first, the thought of buying a friend appears rather odd. The rabbinic commentaries on this phrase, however, make this idea fully comprehensible. A friendship requires an investment of our time and energy. If we want to have a good friend, we must learn to be a good friend, to be supportive when needed, to be constructively critical when appropriate. Friendships require time and the going beyond the boundaries of our individual ego. There are many emotions to overcome such as mutual jealousies, resentments, and insecurities. To "buy" a friend is indeed an expensive proposition.

You are not the only one with faults. Others have faults also. This may seem like a self-evident fact. Yet, when others err, we are often rigid and unforgiving. Forgiving others brings about a great peace of mind. I remember feeling angry at my father for having gotten killed in the war. I was only a young child when he died. As an adult, I understood that it was not his fault for having gotten killed. Many people died. This was a war. But deep within myself, there was a child that had not forgiven him for his leaving. For years I struggled with unresolved feelings and then one night, in meditation, my father came to me in a vision. He told me that he was sorry we had never had the time to grow together. He was with God but his soul was not at rest. I heard the words come out of my mouth as if I were hearing them from some other vantage point, and the words were "I forgive you." I was deeply in meditation, but when the words came, I felt some inner chamber open and a flood of tears poured down my face. When they stopped a great weight had been lifted from me and it has never returned.

Remember that friendship is hands clasped across a chalice of purifying fire.

Where You Sit and What You Wear

Location and clothing are also important. Practice your meditation in the same place each time you meditate. A place builds up energy of its own. The space itself should be uncluttered, clean and have good ventilation. If you want to take a further step in creating the best energy for your meditation space, you may want to learn a little about space arrangement; books on this subject are abundant and the best system I know of is the system of *Feng Shuay*. Have you ever walked into a house of worship, a synagogue, or a church, or a mosque, and felt the powerful energy of the space? As we develop a ritual practice within a space, that space receives and gives back the energy of the ritual. There is also a subtle psychological effect that occurs; we begin to shift in our consciousness as we move toward the space, *even before we enter into it.*

Regarding your meditation space, privacy may also be an important factor. If your situation does not allow for the creation of a separate space for your meditative practice, perhaps an understanding may be reached with friends or family members that a certain corner of a room will be used by you during a specific time. We would like to believe that once we have become experienced in our practice, meditation will be possible under all circumstances. There may be some truth to this. However, the great sages have left us a different message. In India, during the birth of civilizations, the great yogic sages withdrew from these societies to establish mountain communities in the Himalayas. In the Rig Veda, they tell us that it is under these conditions that "...one becomes wise through meditative wisdom."

The same principles apply to the clothes we wear. I am not suggesting that we give credence to the old cliché that "clothes make the man." However, there is much to be said for the idea that clothes play a role in the consciousness we have at a specific time. At our core, we do remain the same and so the work of self-actualization is an internal work, but it is a well documented observation, and a subject of personal experience that a person's sense of self (or perhaps ego) changes with the clothes they are wearing. The clearest example of this is the donning of a uniform. Soldiers feel differently in and out of uniform, and even those around them view the individual differently when he or she is in or out of a uniform. A doorman, a coachman, a waiter, a corporate CEO, all these have their specific uniforms and when they don these clothes, their persona goes through a subtle but distinct transformation.

As Shakespeare observed, all life's a stage and we but players upon it; and in a man's life, he plays many roles. Meditation also has its uniforms. Clothes for meditation should be clean, somewhat loose fitting without any restriction on breath or movement. Natural fibers may also be more consistent with the inner work of meditation. Colors may be of some importance. Each of the energy centers of the body has a corresponding color and thus, the use of specific colors may stimulate a particular energy response in the body and mind.

The Most Important Vitamin

So now we are meditating and we have a location, we are wearing proper clothing and have been taking care of our body with proper hygiene, good food, and correct exercise, *and an insidious and subtle question lurks in the back of the mind.* It is an almost imperceptible voice that at times comes to the fore and demands our attention. And that question, in various forms, goes something like this, "I am doing all these good things. Why am I not happy?" or "Why do I feel a sense of unrest?" To answer this question, I will ask you whether you have taken your vitamins today.

If you have taken them, either in pill form or more naturally through correct nutritional intake, then each of the vitamins and minerals have begun to do their work in strengthening a particular system or function in your body and mind. But happiness and inner peace require one additional vitamin that many people leave out of their diet. Some nutritionists are, in fact, knowledgeable about this vitamin and its importance in a sound nutritional program. The name of this vitamin is vitamin "L." Have you taken your vitamin L today? Do you know what vitamin L is? Vitamin L is love, and with it all our practices and we ourselves are made whole. For, without this vitamin, to what use shall we put all our good works?

If we have a healthy dose of this vitamin daily, we express that quality of the Divine without which the world could not stand. That is the quality of Hesed, of compassion. It is said that God first created worlds with the quality of Judgment and these worlds could not survive in the light of pure judgment. Therefore, God introduced the quality of mercy or compassion., and, thus, creation could continue. There is much emphasis on loving oneself, on taking good care of one self. But this is only half the picture. Without love of others, self-understanding cannot fully blossom.

In our sophisticated society many of the things we speak of may be viewed as archaic or perhaps too simplistic, yet it is these very things, the development of these very qualities, that makes our life-journey and our journey through all other lives an exciting and thrilling experience.

Omar Khayyam wrote in the Rubbayat, "take the cash in hand and leave the beating of a distant drum." And Buddha spoke about *aruparaga*, the attachment to things without form within ourselves. There are many books written to tempt the individual with promises of special powers. My master, Swami Rama, said that there is an insidious voice that lurks in the darker recesses of the mind and this voice has two names: name and fame. What is this voice saying to us? Do this practice and you will become a prophet. The world is waiting for you as the new Messiah. Follow this path and you will see sights and sounds that no one else can see. And why is this important to you? Because then you will become an interesting person and everyone will want to be in your company. People will shower you with rewards and your name will be known around the world.

Do not delude yourself as to the purpose of your self-exploration. It is for mastery of self and liberation from the fetters of illusion.

Taking Responsibility

Adam and Eve are enjoying the fruits in the Garden of Eden, but there is one fruit that is forbidden to them. It is the fruit of the tree of the knowledge of good and evil. Whatever we may think of the fact that this fruit was forbidden to them, the story has other elements of interest. Eve is walking in the garden near the tree of the knowledge of good and evil; the snake apparently is in this tree and asks Eve if God has instructed them (Adam and Eve) not to eat of this tree at the risk of death. Eve then answers that God has said that if they eat of this tree *or touch it*, they would surely die. She has taken it upon herself to add something to the instructions that was not actually said.

With this the snake seizes the opportunity and a Midrash (a teaching) states that the snake bumped into her and caused her to touch the tree. Eve does not die and the snake says, "You see. You touched the tree and you did not surely die. God just wants to keep this knowledge from you because with it you too will become like God." Eve accepts this argument and eats the fruit of the tree and her eyes are opened, so to speak.

Possibly feeling guilty or perhaps not wanting to bear the burden of this act alone, she goes to Adam and offers him the fruit of the tree of the knowledge of good and evil; she tells him that it is a good fruit and that if he eats it his eyes too will be opened and he will be like God. Adam eats the fruit and his eyes are opened.

Now God comes along and Adam and Eve are hiding behind the bushes of the tree. When God asks why they are hiding, they reply that it is because they are naked and they are ashamed. Now God asks Adam how he knows that he is naked. God asks, "Did you eat of the fruit that I told you not to eat?" And here is Adam's great opportunity. But instead Adam replies, *"The woman you gave to me gave me this fruit to eat."* Or in other words, it wasn't my fault. She made me do it. Then God turns to Eve and asks, "Did you give the man the fruit to eat?" And here is Eve's great opportunity. But instead she says, *"the snake told me to eat the fruit saying that I would not surely die but that I would become as God."* Or in other words, it's not my fault. The snake made me do it.

My question, whenever I read this portion of Genesis, is what would have happened if they had accepted responsibility. What if Adam had said, "I'm sorry. I made a mistake. I wasn't thinking. It's true that the woman brought the fruit to me, but you endowed me with free choice and I made a poor choice." And what about Eve? What would our history have been had she said, It's true that the snake seduced me from my better judgment, but you gave me free will and I made a poor choice. I'm sorry. I'll try to do better in the future. I hope that I have learned a lesson from this experience and that you can forgive me." Isn't God's great quality in creation the quality of Hesed (mercy)?

It is this quality of blaming others for our own shortcomings that is inconsistent with a meditative path. We say that we have not achieved this or that because of a string of bad luck, or because someone we placed our trust in had let us down. Or perhaps we can take a British view of these things. I have heard that when it rains in England, the British blame the government. Of course, in the latter case, they do this in good humor. However, it is all too often the case that we find any and every reason for our failure or "bad luck" other than seeing our own role in bringing this about.

There may have been a time when our life was not under our control. This is certainly the case in early childhood. There may indeed be situations throughout our lives that actually warrant our perception that we have not had the freedom to make certain choices. Perhaps we are in jail, or perhaps we are living under a totalitarian regime. Yet, even under such conditions there are significant choices that we can make. And if we are living in conditions of relative freedom, then we must at some point look at our lives with the realization that the present and the future are in our own hands. We are responsible for our actions. We are responsible for our relationships. We are responsible for the positive or negative directions we choose.

To walk on the path of meditation it is necessary to live a life of responsibility for our karma. Master Gotama taught,

> Our bodily conduct shall be purified, clear and open, flawless and restrained, and we will not laud ourselves and disparage others.
> Our verbal conduct shall be purified, clear and open, flawless and restrained, and we will not laud ourselves and disparage others.
> Our mental conduct shall be purified, clear and open, flawless and restrained, and we will not laud ourselves and disparage others.

When knowledge awakens in consciousness, our relation to the external world becomes revealed. Karma, action, is a powerful force that acts upon the formation of our character, and all action is the outcome of the deeper layers of thought and will. These forces act upon one another so that actions form character and character determines the nature of our will. For every action in which we take responsibility, we become strengthened toward greater freedom and self-dependency. For every action in which we disparage others and blame them for the failure of our venture, we add another shackle to the chains that bind us into slavery. And so the rabbis have taught that we go from strength to strength and from weakness to weakness.

Your Practice

We'll conclude our session with a sitting practice and focus on the breath. Observe the physical elements and your mental commitment. And then continue with the practice of breath awareness for one or two minutes. Having established a sense of centeredness, begin the repetition of the following mantra: So...Hum, coordinating the sound So...with the inhalation, and the sound Hum...with the exhalation. Throughout the practice remain with this focus. If you observe that the mind has wandered or been distracted by other thoughts or external stimuli, bring your focus gently back to the So...Hum mantra. Continue with this practice for twenty minutes. At the end of your mantra focus, bring the awareness to the breath and from the breath to the external parts of the body. Thus, we follow certain pathways to the inner dimension of mind, and we follow these same pathways out to the body.

If you are doing this work in a group, ending the session with a group chant is a powerfully energizing and uplifting experience. You may use any chant from any tradition. The only caution I would offer is to use a universal chant rather than one which specifies deities or a specific religious orientation, unless you are in a closed group that shares the same religious ideas.

We have discussed inner principles of being and a set of external behaviors that strengthen and support these inner qualities. As you develop in your perception of the inner light, the Divine, in all people, in all living organisms, in all non-living matter, in every molecule of creation, the power of mind awakens in that place "where all things are possible."

How are we to overcome the darkness that keeps us in chaos and confusion? My master said that we cannot overcome the darkness by confrontation. The way, he said, is to turn on the light. The nature of light is to dispel darkness. There is no conflict. Light is what it is, and in its presence, darkness cannot exist.

In the next sections we will explore some of the fundamental principles that are operative in the universe. These principles are the limited possibilities into which the unlimited quality of expansion takes shape.

Questions for Chapter VI

1. What is the first level of preparation for the work of the spirit?
2. What did Ramban have to say on this subject?
3. What are the conditions related to health that are not within our control? What conditions are somewhat within our control?
4. Explain the relationship of environmental choices and life-style.
5. What are the elements of taking care of your body?
6. Where do we come from physically? And how does this help us make good food choices?
7. Name a basic principle to follow in making good food choices.
8. What food choices can you make from the various food groups that would be consistent with our basic principle?
9. Name the five elements of physical fitness.
10. By what means can one achieve each of these elements?
11. Discuss the importance of location and clothes for meditation.
12. Explain the five elements of fitness.

Chapter VII
Mantra, Yantra, Kundalini and Prana

Your Practice

We begin our session with a sitting practice as in our previous session. Observe the physical elements and the mental commitment. And then continue with the practice of breath awareness with mantra for twenty minutes. Then release the focus on the sound of the mantra, bring the awareness back to the breath, and from the breath to the sitting position of the body. Now gently open the eyes.

In today's session we'll explore the concept of mantra and yantra. Before reading further, take some paper and write your understanding of these terms. Don't be concerned about being "right." We are just getting at the conceptions that we carry around with us and then we'll test these conceptions against the traditions.

A simple understanding of these terms is that mantra relates to sound and yantra relates to light. Both sound and light are, in fact, waves that permeate space. There is scientific theory that maintains that the Universe is composed of sound and light waves. The ancient traditions agree with this theory, and many of these traditions recognize creation as an infusion of these two energies. Webster's dictionary defines sound as, "that which is heard; an auditory effect." As with all our senses, the external experience of sound is a subjective reaction to a waveform, and this reaction is subject to the structure of our senses. The nature of sound, as we know it, comes about from waves moving in air. A well-known example is given of a pebble dropped in a pond of still water. When the pebble enters the water, a series of ripples results that spread out in ever widening circles. If we could follow the journey of the pebble downward through the water, we might also note that there is a continuing displacement of water around the pebble.

Sound waves displace air as the pebble has displaced water. The difference is that the ripples caused by the pebble are only on the surface of the water, whereas the ripples in air caused by a sound continue this ripple effect in all directions. When someone speaks, we hear the sound of his words moving through the air. We cannot see the sound wave, but we experience its pitch, its frequency, its duration, and many other aspects of the sound itself, not to mention the meaning inherent in what is spoken.

What is the quality of air that makes it suitable as a vehicle for sound? Air has two qualities necessary for this effect: elasticity and mass. If we apply pressure to air it will expand. In effect, it will stretch. We can also compress air to some extent by pressing it into a smaller container. Thus, compressed air has a greater density. The quality of mass is easily demonstrated. Our experience verifies the ability of air to move objects. Windmills are pushed by air and they, in turn, generate energy. Sailboats are driven by wind. Storms can generate winds of enough velocity to uproot trees and homes. Or, we may experience a gentle breeze through our hair on a bright spring day.

Because the air has mass, it follows the same laws as other matter, namely, it resists against pressure. And because it has the quality of elasticity, when air resists, it becomes compressed. When the air becomes compressed it becomes

one ripple on the stream and this ripple moves to the next
layer of air compressing it in turn. Each compression leads to
a further compression while previous compressions begin to
decompress – the sound wave that began the process sinking
to the bottom of the pond, so to speak.

A wave (whether sound or light) will travel unobstructed
through air or space until it meets an object that it cannot
pass through. At this point the wave does several things:
it refracts around the object, that is, it curves around the
object; and second, it reflects in various directions. Sound is
a vibration and vibrations have differing frequencies. It is this
quality of frequency that determines the pitch of a sound.

There are many aspects of sound theory that are part of
an expanded discussion on the subject. There is periodicity,
and there is sine wave theory. There are psychological and
physiological considerations. If the reader is interested, this is
a fascinating study and many fine works are readily available
in our libraries.

Physics tells us that the pitch of sound is always related
to the frequency of the repeating waveform. But what is the
nature of sound when there is no air to convey it? We think of
a silent universe, and later in this work we will have occasion
to say that sound is inherent in the Universe. When we use a
mantra it is a repeated sound within the mind (unless we are
chanting). Does sound travel in a space where there is no air
to convey it? Is the mind such a space?

We've seen in our discussion of breath that the yogic model
posits a series of layers or koshas from the inner level of self
to the outer level of annamayakosha, the physical sheath. Can
we say that the self is dropped into life and begins a process
of ripples that move through the universal stream? Pure
thought is a vehicle for sound and light. Musicians "hear"
sounds and then translate these sounds to compositions
or musical performance; artists see color, light and shadow
in their minds as well as in the world around them. We do
not need to be professional musicians or artists. All of us
experience sound and light in our inner world.

What is the "Big Bang" theory of science? Was there an actual heard sound (assuming there was someone to hear it)? Was there an atmosphere to convey this immense sound? East and West occult science teach that the Universe is a composition of Divine Light and Divine Sound.

The Birth of the Universe

Traditional teaching in the great systems of world thought, in Kabbalah, in Hinduism, in Christianity, is that sound preceded light in the process of creation. Remember the words in Genesis,

In the beginning created God, the heaven, and the earth,
And the earth was without form and void
And the spirit of God moved upon the face of the waters
And God said, *let there be light...*

And so we read in the New Testament,

In the beginning was the Word,
and the Word was with God,
And the Word was God

In order to understand the significance of the word "mantra," some explanation of its etymology will be helpful. The root of this word is from the verb-root *man* and it means *to think*; the same root is found in the Sanskrit word *manas* and it means *mind*. The word *mantra* also comes from this root.

We've seen that meditation is really the process of concentration and that it moves through the stages of meditation and self-realization. These latter stages cannot be practiced, but it is mantra that purifies the mind and leads us to *sammadhi* and to *devekut*, union with God.

If we assume a western model, our focus becomes semantic processing. When a word is given, it acts as a "prime". The prime is followed by a target that may be a related word, or it may be an unrelated word. The word may be a non-word. Primes have been shown to influence the efficiency with which we process target words. The interesting thing about primes is that semantic priming seems to occur automatically, even when the individual is ignoring the prime or remains unaware of it. The prime, in fact, may be moving at speeds that make it unrecognizable; even under these circumstances, semantic priming occurs. Based on this view, we might consider that any word may act as a prime and, by extension any word may act as a mantra.

What is a Phoneme?

Now a difficulty presents itself that must be clarified. Can anything be a mantra? What if I were to take the sound of the word "pencil" and repeat this sound until it permeated my mind, until all random thoughts were eliminated. We've said that it could lead me to more efficiently process target words, whether related or unrelated. This relationship is one of shared pathways. Therefore, priming may result from a great number and variety of related words. A word contacts visual, phonological and semantic codes. This entire set of activations is what is referred to as a psychological pathway. But the teaching is that mantra has the power to lead us to transcendence. Could this sound, "pencil," lead me to transcendence?

In order to answer this question, we need to go further in our definition of mantra and so I will offer the following definition that has come down to me from my masters.

*Mantra is that sound **heard** by the most evolved individuals of our species in their moment of deepest communion with the Divine."*

The key word here is "heard." It is a sound that they heard, and not one that they created. This means that the sound pre-existed our creation of sounds. In linguistics, there is a name for such sounds. They are called phonemes. A phoneme is a fundamental unit of sound that exists independently of us. It is a primal sound that exists in the Universe. This, in part, explains the power of mantra to lift us beyond ourselves. If it were our own creation, we would be bounded by the limitation of our own expression. But, as it is inherently part of the Universe, the mantra has the power to lift us beyond ourselves. This is the understanding of the mantra guiding us from the finite to the infinite. We are still dealing with pathways, but these pathways are on a much more primeval level. They are pathways that are the fabric of creation. We move along the strings of the Universe.

The uses of primal sounds for healing and initiation may be traced back to all ancient traditions and all peoples. In modern society also we have discovered the power of sound and we use it within the healing professions. An example of this is the ultrasound machines that are used for diagnostic purposes. Sound is a wave and as a wave it has the power to rearrange molecules.

Were an airplane to fly over your home and break the sound barrier, your dishes and glasses might easily break, things in your home would be dislodged from shelves, and you would become aware of the effects in a number of other ways. Chanting a mantra is to produce a sound outside of oneself and inside of oneself. The vibrations of that sound have the power to pass through objects, to vibrate around tissue and bone, around body organs and blood. The vibrations of a chanted mantra or primal sound have the power to dissolve blockages and liberate energy. They have the power to heal and to make whole. A mantra that is not vocalized also has this power because it is an internalized sound. It is a more subtle sound, but its effects are even more far-reaching because of that very subtlety. It is a sound vibration on the inner sheaths of manomayakosha and vijnanamayakosha.

From another perspective, language itself, although created by people, has the potential for holiness and for bringing great evil into the world. The holy nature of language is expressed through its numerical relationships in Kabbalah. Thus, the word for language is SaFaH, made up of the Hebrew letters Shin, Phey, and Hey; their numerical value totals 385 and this is the same value as the word Shekheenah, the female presence of God on the Earth. It is very clear that language may elevate or tear the fabric of life.

There are primal sounds and there are strings of sounds that represent language. Mantra is generally a string of sounds that is either a word or a sequence of words. I have heard teachers say that knowing the meaning of one's mantra is a hindrance to its effectiveness. Where do our mantras come from? They have been "heard" by sages in various traditions and, as such, they have been heard in the languages of these traditions. Can we say that a yogic sage does not know the meaning of OM, or of OM namo guru dev namo, or of the words of the Gayatri mantra? Does a Jewish sage not know the meaning of Sh'ma Yisrael?

Mantra has four levels: it has a meaning; it has a feeling; it has a presence; and, on its most subtle level, it has sound without sound. The mantra that we will now learn is particularly effective because of its relationship to the flow of the breath.

So...Hum

The mantra that we introduced in our practice is "So... Hum." We have seen that this mantra is coordinated with the breath as follows: *So* is heard with the inspiration, and *Hum* is heard with the expiration. The meaning of this mantra is "that I Am." It is actually a universal mantra and it appears in the traditions of many peoples. In the Chumash, the Five Books of Moses, we read that Moses stood before a burning bush and the voice of God spoke to him out of the fire of the bush. When he received instructions to go back to Egypt to liberate his people, he answered that the people would ask him who it was that sent him as the messenger. The voice of God then says *"Eheeyeh Ki Eheeyeh," I Am That I Am.* This is a So...Hum meditation; a recognition of the unity of sound and breath, and an expression of the Divine at the center of the creation of the Universe.

There are, of course, many other mantras that are available to you, and many of these are not necessarily coordinated with the breath. For example, the mantra OM would not be repeated in consort with the breath. And there is also the question of receiving a personal mantra. This is not essential for developing and having a meditative practice. Many individuals, however, want a personal mantra and if this is your desire, you must find someone who is qualified in giving you such a mantra. Remember our definition of a mantra as a "sound heard in a state of deep meditation." The masters of the esoteric schools will give you a personal mantra if the universe gives your mantra for them to convey to you. It is a sound "heard."

Take a few moments before going on. Close the eyes, establish a good sitting posture, and focus the mind on the breath. Let everything relax and allow the mind to become a little quieter. Now begin to coordinate the breath with the sounds So...Hum. With each inspiration repeat or hear the sound *So...*, and with each expiration repeat or hear the sound *Hum....* Continue with this practice for twenty minutes. Then release the focus on the sound of the mantra, bring the awareness back to the breath, and from the breath to the sitting position of the body. Now gently open the eyes.

And There Was Light

So now we come to the word *Yantra*. Many of you had heard the word mantra and no doubt had some idea of its meaning. Yantra, however, is a less familiar word. Yantra, for our purposes, means "light." It also is representative of a wave--energy in the universe. There are many kinds of yantras. There are mandalas, tatwas, bindus, Tarot cards, the letters of the Hebrew alphabet, and the letters of the Sanskrit alphabet (these two languages are called the holy languages). A yantra may be as simple as a tatwa or a bindu, or it may be complex as a mandala or a Tarot card. In any case, we are dealing with visual images, and the subconscious mind responds more readily to visual images than to any other type of influence.

The power of images and pictures has long been recognized in the esoteric schools and has been taught as a close-held secret throughout the centuries. And so, all the great teachers have taught with parables, with picture stories, because they are available to everyone at different levels. A picture story enters the mind at the conscious and subconscious levels and is not dependent on education or intellect. And so we read in Matthew.

Therefore speak I to them in parables: because they seeing see not; and hearing they hear not; neither do they understand.

Matthew is reaching out to his listeners on a different level. He is trying another way. I want to share with you one more quote from one of the fathers of the psychology movement, Sir Francis Galton. He writes,

The free action of a vivid visualizing faculty is of much importance in connection with the higher processes of generalized thought. A visual image is the most perfect form of mental representation whenever the shape, position, and relation of objects to space are concerned. The best workmen are those who visualize the whole of what they propose to do before they take a tool in their hands.

It is reminiscent of the explanation given by Michaelangelo regarding his sculptures. He said that the sculpture exists in the rock, and his only job is to chip away the surrounding rock to reveal its existence.

Should you wish to explore further this dimension of meditation, namely the use of visual images, I would suggest the use of mandalas or Tarot cards. However, each of these is part of an intricate and deep system of meditation, and I strongly urge you to seek out a qualified teacher to pursue these directions. The use of mandala, tatwa, bindu, and chakra meditation is very much in the Kundalini and Tantra Yoga systems, and the Tarot cards, especially the 22 cards of the major arcana, are part of the Kabbalistic system.

The most common experience of light is a stimulus that enters our consciousness through the eye. This is the experience of external light. In other words, we *see* light.

This concept may appear simplistic; however, we begin with definitions, as we have done in much of this work. From definitions we may move toward deeper understandings. The key words here are eyes and light. What is the eye and what is light? Webster's Dictionary gives the following definitions for these words: **eye**, *the organ of sight or vision*; and, **light**, *that form of radiant energy which stimulates visual perception; anything which has luminosity.*

These, as all definitions, actually raise many additional questions. For example, what is perception? This question, it turns out, is not a simple question at all.

Regarding the external eye, there are three key parts: the pupil, the retina, and the lens. As light is reflected from objects in the surrounding environment, it enters the eye by way of the papillary opening; it is then focused on the lens; from here it proceeds onto the retina and at the retina, this light forms images that are then transmitted to the brain. In the brain, mental patterns are generated and these patterns represent what we perceive.

The external and the internal world are both ruled by the great law of change. There is a continual flow of changing visual images. This is because we move in relation to the world around us, and the world around us is moving in relation to the bodies in our solar system. There is a continuous fluctuation in shades of color and light. There is a continuous change in perspective and distance. There is a continuous change in intensity. Considering all this, it is rather amazing that our perceptions lead us to believe in the constant and the permanent. And yet, that is exactly what the mind, for the most part, does.

The mind does not merely record "reality." The mind creates reality. We assume existence and our perception of it. We assume that what we see is what there is. The world is not only real, but it is real according to our perception of its reality. Here is one more pumpkin that needs to be discarded if we are to walk freely down the path toward the village.

We've had occasion to discuss the scientific view of the Universe. But what is it that science is telling us about our preconceived notions and perceptions? Science is telling us that what we see is only one of many possible realities. Can we see atomic or subatomic particles? Can we see electricity? Can we see magnetism? We know these by their effects, but not because we have any way of directly perceiving their existence. Now, with the advent of technologies, we perceive more than we did just a short time ago. Science has told us that each star vibrates at a certain pitch. This is called the music of the stars. Do we hear this music?

The limitation of our senses is that they are attuned within a very specific range and any stimuli outside of this range is also outside of our perception. Considering this fact, what is amazing is the degree of correctness, of connectedness that exists between our senses and the so-called objective reality. Of course, what we perceive may have little to nothing to do with what we know. It is equally true that although we communicate with our fellow travelers on spaceship Earth, as Buckminster Fuller liked to say, we may never experience a stimulus in the same way as anyone else. By mutual agreement, we have said that we will assume what everyone else assumes. If I see geometrical shapes, we can mutually agree on triangles, rhomboids, squares, lines, points, rectangles, and so on.

One more quality of our perception is important to understand if we are to understand some of the teachings regarding yantra. That is the mind's need to place things in relationship to other things. There is the object and there is its context. There is the figure and there is the ground. Unlike sound (mantra), which is distinctly linear and moving across time, our perception of light is of a different nature. With light, we are seeing space and therefore if figures are moving across a landscape, the landscape appears stationary. It is a constant against which we determine the movement of the figures. This is, of course, not accurate. Both are in motion, but in relation to one another, one appears in motion and one appears stationary. It is the same example of a man in a moving train. The surrounding countryside appears to be moving by while he may have the feeling that he is standing still. He, in fact, *is standing still inside* the train. It is an illusion of movement and a difference between perception and knowledge.

With this understanding, we may say that a parable, a visual image, becomes the figure, and the thought-pictures and emotion-pictures that are the continuous flow of the mind become the ground. It is a means of concentrating the mind. With the continued practice and refinement of visualization, our ability to see inwardly grows, and with it grows our ability to shape external reality through the power of the subconscious level of the mind. The yantra and the background are both in motion, but the background continues to flow by while we perceive the illusion of the constancy of the figure that is the yantra. Ultimately, the illusion must be released for the attainment of kaivalya.

The benefits of a yantra are best realized by its repetition over a set period of time. Taking the two systems that have many complex yantras, the kundalini yoga system and the Kabbalah, a good practice is to take a yantra from these traditions and concentrate on it for about a week. After this week, continue with the next yantra until you have gone through the system. Still, this is external concentration and the practice needs to be internalized. Therefore, after gazing at the yantra for a brief time, close your eyes and see in as much detail as possible each element of the yantra. When utilizing visualizations, allow yourself to feel each element physically as well as emotionally.

The Heart's Wounds

At this time, we will practice one visualization to better understand this technique. A visualization may take a number of forms; we'll use one that I received from a teacher several years ago. I particularly like it and would like to know its original source to properly credit this wonderful imagery. So, here it is. The teacher who shared it called it the Wounds of the Heart. It is a way to clear the heart of many things that we carry around that would best be discarded. At this time, sit up straight, yet relaxed. Focus your awareness on the breath for about one minute. Allow the breath to become deep, smooth, gentle and continuous (minimizing any hesitations in the breath). Now, bring your attention to the center of the chest and unzip the front of the chest. Remove the heart and hold it in your hands. Observe the heart carefully for any wounds you may have received. Review in your memory any hurts that are still with you. You now observe that there are arrows through the heart in all the places where the hurt is locked away. At this time, break off the front stems of these arrows and pull the arrows out from the other side.

Now take these broken pieces of arrows and toss them

away behind you. You now become aware of having a golden-blue healing ointment and you massage it into all the places in the heart where the arrows have been. As you continue with this process, begin to feel the strength and the perfect rhythmic beating of the heart. Now, replace the heart into the center of the chest and zip-up the front of the chest. Bring the awareness back to the breath. Take several slow and gentle breaths, and gently open the eyes.

Remember our story about freedom early on in these talks. Well, we can't get through life without hurts. You might use the phrase, "it comes with the territory." But holding on to the hurts is another matter. Often we get quite comfortable with our hurts; they seem to serve some purpose for us. The truth is that holding on to them serves no good purpose at all. Get rid of the pumpkin on your head.

When a fire is made, two energies are liberated: warmth and light. Each of these has a vibration level. Light is the finer vibration of the two. When the Big Bang occurred, matter exploded outward and light was liberated. At the core of creation, there is light. And so Jesus taught, "do not hide your light beneath a bushel. Let your light shine."

Light, like sound, has preexisted us. It is a name for God, but it is only another vessel, albeit a finer vessel. Our language contains sayings that hint at the supernal nature of light. We say, "I have seen the light." We understand, we perceive, we are enlightened, we are elevated to a new consciousness or we have seen the inner truth of a thing. Spiritual awakening is equated with a coming into the light. We refer to inspired knowledge as divine illumination, and this illumination awakens the "prayer of the heart."

So, can any light be a yantra? I leave this question for you.

Your Practice

We'll conclude our session with sitting meditation. At this time, observe the physical elements and the mental commitment. And then continue with the practice of breath awareness. With each inspiration repeat or hear the sound *SO*; and with each exhalation repeat or hear the sound *HUM*; continue with this practice for twenty minutes. After twenty minutes of mantra meditation, release the sound of the mantra and bring the awareness back to the breath in its simple form. From the breath, become aware of the physical body in space. How is your body positioned? How are your legs and arms placed? How is the torso and head balanced? Take a brief journey through the body at this time and if there is any tension anywhere in the body, try to release it now. And now, either open the eyes gently or proceed as below.

If you are doing this work in a group, ending the session with a group chant is a powerfully energizing and uplifting experience. You may use any chant from any tradition. The only caution I would offer is to use a universal chant rather than one which specifies deities or a specific religious orientation, unless you are in a closed group that shares the same religious ideas.

During the coming week, continue to incorporate a relaxation practice and a twenty-minute sitting practice with mantra.

What did you discover in thinking about the question of yantra? Fire is the earliest form of light that we were able to control. Was there no light in the Universe before we discovered fire? And what of the fire within our control? The Hebrew word for man is ISH, spelled Aleph, Yod, Shin. The Hebrew word for woman is Isha, spelled Aleph, Shin, Hey. Both words contain the letters Aleph and Shin. One word contains a Yod, the other a Hey. Yod and Hey represent one of the names of God; it is the creative aspect of God. Aleph and Shin spell the word for fire. Commentary explains that when a man and woman keep an aspect of the Divine in their relationship, their fire is creative. But if the Divine presence is removed, the fire is consuming.

Questions for Chapter VII

1. What biblical references refer to mantra and yantra?
2. What is the etymology of the word *mantra*?
3. What is the relationship of mantra to our understanding of meditation?
4. Can any sound be a mantra? If the answer is no, then why not?
5. What is a phoneme? And what has this got to do with mantra?
6. Does mantra have healing power? How so?
7. Explain the So...Hum mantra.
8. What is a yantra? Name the different kinds of yantra.
9. Explain why many of the great teachers have taught with parables.
10. What did Matthew, Sir Frances Galton, and Michaelangelo share in their concept of using the power of pictures?

Chapter VIII
Meditation in Motion

Moving Meditation

Moving meditation at first appears to be the very opposite of sitting meditation, and there is, in fact, much to be said for the essential difference, but on a deeper level we perceive that there is no such state as perfect stillness in this universe. Everything is flowing, moving, changing, exploding or shifting. We sit still, but our breath continues, our heart and lungs are still at work, all body processes are continuously at work. The cells, atoms and molecules in our bodies continue their dance.

If this is the case, where is the stillness that we have spoken about? The stillness that we experience is in the mind. And so we may extend our inquiry and ask whether this stillness is available when the body is in motion or only when we are at rest and quieting the body by a minimizing of external motion.

The answer is obvious. There are many traditions in which dance is a form of meditation. There is dervish dancing. There is Chassidic dancing. Most native peoples have some form of ritual dance that has elements of ecstatic experience. Even modern disco dancing with its pulsating rhythms can lead the dancer into an altered state. Although the loudness of the music may not be to everyone's taste, disco dancing has all the elements of creative movement. There is spontaneity and originality. Within the parameters of structured movement, the dancers express their individuality.

There are, of course, more formal patterns of dance that draw on stylized traditions. This is the way most dance is communicated and taught. We observe the movements of a master (Tai Chi or Ballet) and we copy these movements as best we can.

Dance, like other forms of expression, evolves and transforms itself to reflect the expressions of time and place. But what did it evolve from? Were we always dancers? Did Cro-Magnon man dance? Apparently, some enormous shift took place some 35,000 years ago. At this time, there was a sudden leap in evolution in which the brain mass of prehistoric man dramatically increased. This fact has been the basis of intense debate and speculation in the scientific community. Some writers have even suggested that we were visited by aliens from space and that these aliens co-habited with the local higher life-form, man. This then led to the development of a new species with the capability to develop civilizations. It is not necessary for us to consider this and other theories about the change. It is, however, noteworthy.

At this point in the development of Homo Sapiens visual images became a prominent mode of expression, and these images took form in religious and cult rituals. Religion, theater, and dance were not separate, but worked together to express early man's perception of the Universe and of his world. This means of expression sought through symbol and myth to express something that language could not contain. And so, the dancers became gods and goddesses, and by this humanization of elemental forces, the creation was understandable.

Why include a chapter on moving meditation? The answer is simple. Just as there are different diets for different people, so there are different modes of meditation. Not everyone is well suited for sitting meditation. Some people discover *kaivalya* through movement. For these individuals, the higher realms of *devekut* are accessible along this path.

William Butler Yeats said that dance is the closest form to God. God, we say, is the wellspring, the source of all things. Therefore, God is the source of movement. Some years ago, I introduced spontaneous rhythmic movement into several of my yoga classes. I combined these movements with guided visualizations, or at least, the bare bones of guided visualizations, relying on each participant to fill in their own story line. After the dance, sharing our experience, many of us felt that we had connected to a sacred aspect of reality.

There are many traditional forms. There is classical dance and folk dance. There is ballroom dance and native dance that exhibits ritual elements. But, no matter what the form, when dance takes us to the source of itself, we pass beyond the forms. I am not a great fan of ballet. I have always found it too rigid, too structured. And yet, when I watched Mikhail Baryshnikov dance I was totally mesmerized. It literally appeared to me that he had somehow mastered gravity and the only reason he did not totally fly was to preserve our illusion. I remember thinking what I had often thought before, that it is not the particular form, but the individual who somehow utilizes the form yet passes beyond it. The difference is between mastering of the techniques and total self-expression.

In the middle of the eighteenth century there was a rabbi named the Baal Shem Tov, the Master of the Good Name. He lived at a time when religious worship had become a dreary affair in which those at prayer bemoaned their fate and their history. Prayer had become an opportunity for sadness and tears. The Baal Shem Tov brought a different teaching. He said that this was not the way to worship God. He said that regardless of external circumstances, when we worship God it ought to be with joy, with song and with dance. He was the founder of the Hassidic movement, and so when Hassidim dance, their dance is an expression of sacred ecstasy.

The Baal Shem Tov was not teaching something new. He awakened the memory in the worshippers of another way to touch the Divine, a way that was ancient beyond the structures of civilization and societies. As we begin to dance and to harmonize our movement to the internal rhythms of our body, and, by extension, to the internal rhythms of the Universe, the boundaries between concentration, meditation, and liberation diminish, and then disappear. There is only the north star of our metaphysical universe, One Mind, One Law, One Principle, One Substance, and I am one with all there is. The intellectual knowledge of this truth disappears into its experience, an experience that is not contained in language.

In dance we realize the principle of yang and yin, the duality in all creation. Through dance, we go beyond the duality to its oneness through the transformations of constant change. We speak about a cosmic breath, about God's exhalation and God's inhalation; we understand that there is growth and there is decay; there is up and there is down; there are inner and outer conditions of body and mind. Much of this perception is the result of the boundaries of our perception. In movement and dance, we discover the principle of tension and release.

Every change in movement involves a change in tension and release patterns. Superficially, we speak of this pattern as a physical pattern, but it is far more than this. There are many forces at work in all our activities; this is equally true when we dance. There are spiritual and emotional/intellectual forces, as well as physical ones at work. There is reciprocity in that these forces not only work on us, but as we explore our potentials, we learn about these forces and about ourselves. Tension and relaxation are always present in every movement. As one set of muscles relaxes, a different group of muscles becomes tense. There is a balancing, a neuromuscular coordination that is taking place.

Everything in the Universe is movement. Sound is a waveform. Light is a waveform. But, is all movement dance? Formally, it is not. Yet, all movement may be said to be a part of a cosmic dance. The seed that breaks forth from the soil and begins to sprout, the sprout that grows and begins to bud, the bud that opens to a flower, and the flower that withers and falls into the soil is a dance. The deer that runs through the forest is a dance. The hunter and his arrow are a dance. The movement of the stars and the heavens has been referred to as a dance and symphony. As you walk through the street, begin to observe people closely. Study their movements. See how one person runs for a bus, another stands shifting his weight back and forth, possibly waiting for someone. Watch how different people walk and sit and stand. Observe the workers at their jobs. If you look closely, you may see the incredible and phenomenal cosmic symphony and dance that is taking place every moment. Where is God? Look around you and see for yourself.

Using imagery in movement, there is only one requirement, and that is the willingness to "let go." During most of our activities, a certain degree of restraint and inhibition is appropriate. However, there are times when we need to let go of our inhibitions completely. It is not an easy thing to do. We hold on to our core, that is, our beliefs, our self-image, our fears, and so on. The dance movements that we refer to are spontaneous, creative, and original. There is no core, only constant flux. The energy moves within us and through us. It is transcendent, outside and around us; it is immanent – at the center of every cell in our body. It is the three aspects of soul that Kabbalah says are the light within man; and it is the two aspects of soul that Kabbalah says are the light outside of man. This is a connection to infinity.

When you dance to discover creative movement, the only thing that matters is your space. It is your space, your body in your own space, and no one else around you. You may be in a room full of people, but when you allow the energy to flow through you, there is only you in your space. There are no questions, no statements; there is no self-conscious perception. There is only you and you are unique.

You might choose a more technical approach, that is, a style that is formalized as a tradition. There are many such styles and they are based on form and substance. Their substance is their physical aspect, their specific steps and sequences, and their form is the energy pattern around which they have formed. The form is their internal dimension. Besides traditional folk dance and formal classical dance, there are the many dance forms that are part of the martial arts tradition. When you see an Aikido class or a Tai Chi class, can you not recognize their choreography? It is a more rigorous route to self-expression, but like any form of meditation, it is a discipline. And the consistent and persistent practice of a discipline leads to its deeper experience. Nevertheless, at some point in your progress with this discipline, it must become your own; it must be an expression of your personal vision.

For formal training, there are many fine schools and teachers that you may wish to seek out. For our purposes, as a brief introduction, to this method of meditation, we will focus on spontaneous, creative movement with the use of imagery. The following exercises are meant only to get you started in the exploration of dance as a means of discovering your self.

The Tree

Stand with your legs about the distance of your hips and the knees softly bent. Allow yourself to sink into the bottoms of your feet. The arms are held loosely at the sides of the body and the torso is erect but relaxed. As you focus on the following visualization, let your knees slightly straighten and bend in a continuous rhythm. Do the following practice with your eyes closed.

Imagine that you are a tree and that your roots are extending downward through the bottoms of your feet. Follow the roots downward as they pass through the floor of your space (or the earth, if you are outdoors). Feel or imagine the roots passing through the upper, soft layer of topsoil. Now the roots come to a deeper layer of earth, a rocky layer that is hard and resistant. The roots begin to break through this layer finding their way sometimes through and sometimes around this rocky layer. The roots move ever downward, rooting deeper into the earth. Your roots now break through this rocky layer and come to the next layer down. It is a layer of fire, a river of molten fire. The roots sink into this molten heat and the heat begins to rise through the roots. It rises through the rocky layer and through the soft topsoil. It rises through the bottoms of your feet and up into the legs. This fire from a deeper layer of earth now moves throughout your body melting any blockages with its intense heat. It energizes every cell of the body with the heat and the nutrients that it brings from the earth.

As this heat rises through the body, allow your arms to float upward on its energy. Imagine that your arms are the branches of this tree and the tree is reaching up toward the sky. It is day and the branches draw warmth from the sun downward to meet the warmth from the earth. You now become aware that you are part of a great forest. There are gentle winds that move through the forest and sway your branches. Let your whole body move freely except the bottoms of the feet. Let all your senses awaken to the great forest around you. Take in every fragrance, every sound; feel every breeze and sensation.

The day is now waning and there is a full moon rising. The moon is an orb of cool, silver light. With the coming of night, the branches lower and the tree begins to sleep until the coming of day. Feel or imagine the roots now rising from the molten layer of earth, rising through the rocky layer of earth and through the soft topsoil until they retract once again into the bottoms of the feet. Begin to slow the external rhythmic movement of your body, but keep the internal rhythm fully awakened. Bring your body to a stop and focus the mind on your time and place in the great forest.

You now begin an evolution from a tree to a human being. Become fully aware of your present time and space, of yourself in this time and space. As you open your eyes, remember that you were once a tree and remember every feeling and sensation that you had in the great forest of trees.

If you choose to explore meditation in movement, become creative. Make up your own visualizations. Take a trip to ancient Egypt and dance along the shores of Nile in the season when its waters overflow the banks and fertilize the earth. Walk into a wood of cypress trees and join their dance after establishing your own dance. Dance on a beach in Hawaii and let your senses awaken to the saltiness of the sea, and to the sound and rhythm of the waves.

Another exercise may be done in a group and that is the circle, which is described below.

The Circle

Stand in a circle with every participant having enough space to move freely. Use rhythmic music with a steady drumbeat; at first we stand and listen to this rhythm. We begin to take it inside of us and we begin to move to this beat. As you move to the external beat of the music, begin to take it further inside of you, to discover its connection to your own inner rhythm. In this setting you discover that your movements are at first mechanical, and somewhat more inhibited than when you were moving alone. You may discover a greater need to exercise control. This is a good time to remember the witness stance of meditation. Be a witness to your movements and relinquish any sense of meaning or purpose. It is a time for self-discovery.

In this dance, the entire body is in motion. There is no rooting in place. As the dance continues, perhaps it will lead to chanting, perhaps to togetherness or perhaps to isolation. There is no one way. The circle will evolve from the individuals that compose it. Whatever it is, let yourself be open to what it has to give.

You see there are no boundaries here. Let your imagination be your guide. At some point, these images fade and there is only you and the energy that is moving inside you, and that is sacred dance.

Conclusion

Thank you for sharing this learning process with me. We've come on a long journey together in these few weeks of practice. Distance is measured in many different ways and there is travel outside of time and space. The purpose of this little book has been to introduce you to a tradition and a practice that is perhaps more significant at this juncture in history than ever before.

We may ask why these teachings were guarded and not widely disseminated. Tradition, after all, teaches that the earlier generations were on a higher level than we are. This is stated in the teaching of Lao Tse when he says that "...the nearer the source, the purer the stream." Earlier generations and earlier prophets reported direct experience of the Divine, and yet these teachings were not part of the knowledge of the general populace. Today, these esoteric and occult teachings are very widespread. Why is that?

The story is told of a king who had a young son and this young son became seriously ill. The king called in the royal physicians and they examined the boy. They then came to the king and informed him that the boy had a rare illness and that there was only one known cure; this cure, they said, was a rare jewel that, when powdered down and given as a drink, would cure the prince. The king praised their work in determining the illness and the cure and instructed them to get this rare jewel and cure the young prince.

The physicians, however, were not able to do this. They explained to the king that they did not know where this jewel might be found. In fact, they knew of only one such jewel in existence and it was the crown jewel in the crown of the king.

The king now said that this would be impossible. The crown jewel was the essence of the crown and if it were destroyed, the crown too would be destroyed. He instructed them to try other means.

Over the next several months, the physicians tried many cures, but they were all to no avail and the young prince became more and more ill until he was at the point of dying. The physicians now came back to the king and they related the prince's condition saying that he was going to die and that they were not certain that there was anything that could save him at this point.

When the king heard this, he gave them his crown and told them to take the crown jewel, to do whatever they had to do, but to save the life of the prince.

And so the question is raised, why did the king not give the crown jewel in the beginning, and why is he willing to give it now? At first the young prince was not yet so ill, and the king was hopeful that the physicians would find some other way of curing him. To destroy the crown jewel would be to destroy the symbol of the kingdom and so the king was willing to try other ways. But when it became apparent that there were no other cures, that the crown jewel was the only means of saving the young lad's life, the symbol was only of secondary importance.

The story is an allegory and the crown jewel is the nistar, the hidden teachings, the esoteric sciences. These were the domain of a priesthood and of the priestess societies of the ancient world. In the west and the east, these sciences were handed down by master to disciple, by teacher to student. The people were closer to God in their simple faith and belief. Today, we place our faith and belief in material science as we continue on the road of separating matter and spirit. It is a time when essential truths are more significant than ever before.

I hope that you have learned about yourselves from our journey and that you will choose to continue on the inner path. I believe that we come into this world with a natural inclination toward inner experience. As children and adolescents, we have tremendous power of imagination. Our images are clear and complete. We see figures in clouds. We read the shapes of earth and trees and rocks. The waves on the ocean are objects of focus for our deepest reflections and imaginings.

Then, comes the bombardment of external stimuli, the growth of an information glut. Today, this is true more than ever. We are assailed by television, movies, the Internet – these and other media give us predetermined and mostly artificial images. Our inner vision becomes distorted, and worse still, it becomes dark. We have no visions, no imaginings. The colors have faded; the shapes are no longer in the clouds and the earth. The trees and the rocks have no messages to give us.

The messages are still there. We have only to listen.

GLOSSARY

Abdominal	Relating to the abdomen, the front lower part of the trunk of the body.
Allegory	A description that conveys a different meaning from that which is expressed.
Buddha	A person who has attained Buddhahood; a representation of Gautama Buddha (the founder of Buddhism).
Chakra	A whirling vortex, a wheel, a disc. It is a psychic energy center that activates both the body and the mind.
Concentration	To concentrate is to bring to a common center or point of union; to direct toward one object by removing non-essentials; to reduce to a state of great strength and purity.
Conscious	Perceiving, apprehending, or noticing with a degree of controlled thought or observation.
Consciousness	The totality of conscious states of an individual; the quality or state of being aware of something within oneself.
Devekut	Gluing; to be glued to (God).

Dhamma	Buddha's teaching and ministry.
Diaphragm	A dome-shaped muscular partition between chest and abdomen.
Didactic	Designed to instruct.
Dissolution	Disintegration; death; breaking down into component parts. Dispersion.
Divine	Proceeding directly from God.
Esoteric	Designed for and understood by the specially initiated alone; relating to knowledge that is restricted to a small group.
Evolution	A process of change from a lower, simpler state to a higher, more complex state. A process of change in a certain direction.
Exegesis	Interpretation and illustration of Scripture.
Gravitation (gravity)	A force manifested by acceleration toward each other of two free material particles or bodies or of radiant-energy quanta.
Hokhma	Wisdom
Imminence	Being within; being at the core.
Involution	The act or instance of enfolding or entangling. To return to a former state; a regressive alteration.
Jing	The substance that moves slowly in the process of change.
Kabbalah	A system of Jewish and Hermetic theosophy, mysticism, and thaumaturgy; belief in creation through emanation; a cipher method of interpreting Scripture.
Kaivalya	Liberation
Karma	Action
Kavannah	Intent
Khaya	The light that emerges from wisdom.
Kosha	Sheath

Liberation	To set free from domination by a foreign power.
Mantra	Relates to sound; a mystical formula of invocation; that sound heard by certain individuals in the moments of deepest meditation.
Maya	Temporal; related to time and space.
Meditation	To meditate is to dwell on anything in thought, to turn or revolve any subject in the mind; it is close or continued thought.
Metaphor	A figure of speech which makes an implied comparison between things which are not literally alike.
Metaphysics	A division of philosophy that includes ontology (concerned with the nature and relations of being) and cosmology (the Universe as an orderly system; deals with the origin, structure, and space-time relationships of the Universe).
Mezzuzah	A small case containing Scriptural passages and attached to the doorpost of a Jewish home as a sign and reminder of the Jewish faith. The passages contained are Deut. 6:4-9 and 11:13-21.
Monastic	As in seclusion or ascetic simplicity; learning by experience.
Niglah	Revealed knowledge
Nistar	Hidden knowledge
OM	In the Yogic philosophy, the holiest of holy words, the mother of all names and forms, the word out of which the whole universe is supposed to have been created. The symbol of God; the symbol of reality.
Phonology	Study of speech sounds; phonetics.
Physiology	A branch of biology that deals with the functions and activities of life or of living

	matter; the organic processes and phenomena of an organism or any of its parts.
Prana	Life energy
Pranayama	Control of the life-energy
Psychotherapy	The treatment of mental or emotional disorder or of related bodily ills by psychological means.
Qi	The energy associated with all movement in the Universe; that out of which the life force emerges.
Relaxation	To make less tense or rigid; a diminution of tension.
Sammadhi	Higher consciousness; self-actualization
Scholastic	One who adopts academic or traditional methods of acquiring knowledge.
Self	The union of elements that constitute the individuality and identity of a person; the realization of an abstraction; the entire person of an individual.
Semantic	Pertaining to the meaning of words; a branch of linguistic research concerned with studying meaning and changes in meaning of words.
Simile	A figure of speech using some point of resemblance observed to exist between two things that differ in other respects.
So...Hum	That I Am
Subconscious	The mental activities below the threshold of consciousness.
Svadhyaya	Self-study
Symbol	Something that represents something else. To invest ordinary objects with imaginary meanings
Tefillin (phylacteries)	Two small square leather boxes containing parchment inscribed with Scriptural

passages; traditionally worn on the left arm and on the center of the forehead by Jewish men during morning prayers.

Thorax
A part of the body between the neck and the abdomen; chest cavity containing the heart and lungs.

Torah
The body of wisdom and law contained in Jewish Scripture and other sacred literature and oral tradition.

Transcendent
Beyond the limits of ordinary experience; being beyond the limits of all possible experience and knowledge. Being beyond the Universe and material existence.

Yama
Restraints

Yantra
Relates to light. A mystical formula of invocation; a visual image, usually a glyph, representing archetypes or foundational structures in the Universe.

Yoga
A Hindu philosophy teaching the suppression of all activity of body, mind, and will, in order that the self may realize distinction from them and attain liberation.

Yug
Sanskrit root of the word Yoga meaning union.

420354

Made in the USA